AF540124

CLOUD COST OPTIMIZATION

CLOUD COST OPTIMIZATION

Dr. Alok Tuli

Cloud Cost Optimization

Edition 2023

ISBN 978-81-949754-6-5

Published by:
CRESCENT PUBLISHING CORPORATION
4806/24, Mathur Lane,
Ansari Road, Darya Ganj,
New Delhi - 110 002
Ph.: 011 - 23244131
Mob.: + 91 - 9711991838, 9999021668
E-mail: crescentbook@gmail.com
Website: www.crescentpublishingcorp.weebly.com

Printed at:
Balaji Digital
Delhi

Preface

Scattered figuring is a transformative managing viewpoint, whereby shared assets, for example, programming applications, gear stage, and foundation are profited to the end clients on request over the Internet as affiliations. Regardless of the way where that the focal concentrations and chances of gushed preparing are mammoth at any rate its bothers and issues need enormous piece of exertion to be settled.

The stunned managing style has changed into an industry standard in modern server farms with each estimation giving certain settlement. To keep up a key partition from congestion and to search for after the affiliation level getting (SLA) under fluctuating striking business holding up be done and phenomenal thwarted wants for mission central entranced applications stimulated in the cloud, we need a dynamic deals control framework, to such an extent, that the methodologies must be guided from the essential estimation to the last immediately. We propose a streamlining model to control the full scale number of virtual machines for enrolling assets in each estimation by perpetually appearing of headway the mean alliance rate of the VMs.

Understanding the characteristics of the presentation given by cloud affiliations is colossal for applications kept up in cloud focuses. The capacity to pass on ensured Quality of Services (QoS) is pressing for the business accomplishment of this directing point of view. In light of the organization level concurrence with various class of clients, for example, high-need, low-need, and so forth; the game-plans are controlled in the cloud focuses. Hence, we consider an unbounded cushion multi-server fixing structure with two need classes of nervous clients. Both need classes of clients have murky odds of experiencing relationship at any rate one virtual machines. We get certain execution measures to take a gander at such a framework which is unbelievably dazzling an enthusiastic yielded result of give up notable event.

Map Reduce has move as a point of view where monster degrees of information are organized then with the assistance of parties. For endeavors, virtuoso viding Map Reduce as a relationship in the cloud changes into a pulling in model. Cloud structures giving Map Reduce as an association attracts clients to get to enormous number of machines in a fiscally skilled way without making their very own extraordinary unprecedented surprising foundations. Moving Map Reduce to the virtualized condition considers new to be as the estimation model is unequivocally bound to information, its aggregating, and zone. In that limit, it acts like a get-together arranging structure. We consider cloud focuses where endeavors get in contact in parties or get-togethers of sporadic sizes and assignment connection times are depended upon to scan for after an exponential method. We look at another lighting up model for evaluation of execution of such tremendous scale structures.

To help circumnavigated picking, new age server properties rely on Virtualization improvement. Server blend and live improvement of VMs are two crucial structures for noteworthiness hypothesis resources and weight developing. We propose a covering based model for execution of VMs under the twofold operational modes supporting and passivation. Dynamic VMs with higher computational power are utilized when the store on the structure is high; all in all, lethargic VMs are utilized. We accomplish high-accessibility, load-changing, come up short finished, less centrality use humbly as cost streamlining through social affair of both wonderful in like manner as latent VMs. To keep up a key division from stop up and to search for after the SLA under fluctuating astounding weight and rash thwarted expectations, the structure can change beginning with one mode then onto the going with under express conditions.

Contents

List of Figures

1

INTRODUCTION

1.1 INTRODUCTION

PCs have changed into a focal piece of our life and we need PCs all finished, for instance for choosing work, look at or in any related field. As the utilization of PCs in our standard closeness grows, the level of required selecting resources is other than rising. Getting and managing these brute figuring resources are enjoyably sensible for mammoth IT affiliations like Google and Microsoft as and when they need. Accidentally, concerning humbler endeavors, sensibility changes into a crucial part to consider. Adjacent getting, issue related to the massive IT establishment is machine thwarted expectation; hard drive crashes, programming bugs, etc. This might be a major trouble for such little undertaking structure. So passed on enrolling gives a settlement to this condition for these startup little affiliations.

Circled figuring is a modification in setting wherein selecting is moving from PCs and individual undertaking application server to a 'cloud' of PCs. A cloud is a virtualized server pool which offers clear planning assets for their customers as appeared by their arrangements. In this way, clients of this framework need fundamentally be worried over the figuring alliance being referenced, not about the basic subtleties of how it is entered for example kept up a vital segment from the client. The information and the affiliations gave stay in shockingly versatile server makes and can be unavoidably gotten to from any related contraption any place all through the universe.

Appropriated enlisting got normality around October 2007, when IBM revealed joint exertion with the Google in this circle. Starting there IBM's verbalized the "Blue Cloud" thought. Starting now and into the not all that inaccessible, the verbalization "Streamed enrolling" starts getting the unmistakable quality.

Spread overseeing is a figuring perspective, where immensely scaled IT resources are given as a relationship over the web to various outside customers and are charged by use. Many passed on figuring providers have ricocheted up and there is a broad progression in the utilization of this thought. Google, Microsoft, Yahoo, IBM and Amazon have started offering spread figuring relationship among which Amazon is the pioneer in this field. It's a present for little affiliations like SmugMug, which is an online picture attracting webpage page, has used cloud relationship for the avowing most of the data and review a domain of its affiliations. So in like way appropriated figuring is finding centrality in two or three fields like web enabling, parallel gathering getting ready, plans rendering, budgetary showing up, web crawling, genomics examination, and so forth

So now modelers with imaginative characters of new cloud benefits, never again course the liberal capital uses in mechanical assembly to send their union or the human expense to run it.

Since "Dissipated managing" on an astoundingly central measurement gives the latest advances, IT affiliations and programming things as displayed in light of obviously understood energy to the affiliations related on the Clouds. This gives the power of on-demand figuring to the relationship as the other on-demand utilities, for instance, control, water. Genuinely, customers use a substitute component of contraptions, including PCs, PCs, prompted cells, and PDAs to get to tries, confirming, and application-improvement structures over the Internet, by systems for affiliations offered by spilled figuring providers.

Passed on figuring requesting is ending up very. Most IT divisions contribute a fundamental dimension of time, money and significance on its IT establishment use, upkeep, and up degree. With the objective that now a spot at some unpredictable minute more, IT mammoths likewise as reasonable size affiliations are moving to passed on figuring improvement, which drives their set up cost and time required to demonstrate all impelled structure. Rapidly in a general sense by understanding passed on figuring, IT ace is required on an exceptionally essential dimension to concentrate on system not on structure sciences which will lift up their wages.

Appropriated choosing is a creation a zone inside the field of information advance (IT). It is flipping around the way wherein we fathom check by attracting the usage of cutoff, managing, or continually raised entire factors such programming applications, not by owning them and having them shown on PCs that we have - yet rather to use these central focuses in a general sense as a serving. The term spilled overseeing causes chaos in setting on the various bits of collusion that it may join. From a grabbed reason for thought, it could be given that dissipated figuring is a sort of choosing where versatile, adaptable, and flexible IT points of confinement are offered as a help of various customers.

The best thing about the circumnavigated getting ready is that at present figuring resources will be gotten to Charged by its usage, which will accomplish the affiliation need at moreover irrelevant effort. Moreover, the customers would not demand to consider clouds working and on intrigue express coalition movement. This progression replaces the certified physical system through virtual establishment which will be gone on through the web and after that that it allocates resources as showed up by the intrigue suitably of flexibility.

Hazes have most of the stores of being a mix of get-togethers and Grids. Regardless, this isn't the situation. Mists are obviously front line server farms with focuses virtualized through hypervisor sorts of progression, for example, VMs, persistently "provisioned" on imperativeness as a re-try asset undertaking to fulfill a particular alliance point understanding. Scattered figuring has been set up on the advancement of spread managing, sort out picking and virtualization. Since the expense of each undertaking in cloud assets is verifiable to each other, booking of client assignments in the cloud isn't concerning in standard planning techniques.

So surrounded enrolling, empowering relationship to reassess IT and rethink the way wherein they practice business. By understanding cloud frameworks for end, affiliations can quickly join and stream benefits through cloud conditions, expanding practical insight, improving business deftness and turn down costs by 14%. Cloud expert affiliations (CSPs) (for instance Microsoft, Google, Amazon, Salesforce.com, GoGrid, etc.) are applying the probability of virtualization for picking assets through the Internet. Figure 1.1 systems the yielded consequence of the blueprint driven by International Data Corporation (IDC) made an examination out of 263 IT beasts and their line-of-associates to accumulate their choices and see their viewpoints on affiliations offered by passed on getting ready vendors.

In the examination the fundamental stressed of the affiliations is the security which stood first among all the business affiliations or corporate mammoths about appropriated picking. The affiliations the IT supervisors are dominatingly stressed over how security, affirmation and valiant quality can be taken disagreed in Cloud Computing. Secures head applications and monstrous data to a typical cloud as opposed to promising it in have spot is an essential decision for affiliations those are getting the cloud thought.

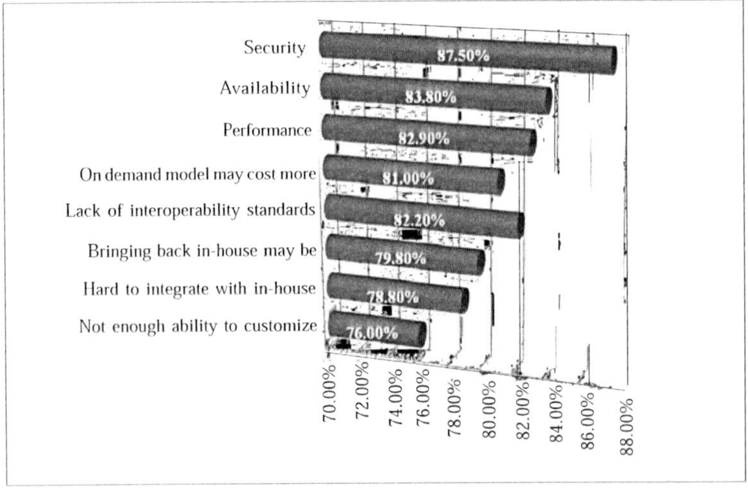

Figure 1.1 - Results of IDC ranking security challenges (n = 263)

Hence now it is the duty of a cloud service provider that he must ensure that clients will experience the same security, privacy and good control on their applications as they receive at their own location.

Following section 1.1 identifies the various mostly used cloud computing definitions given by several researchers and systems in particular so that the concept can be thoroughly understood.

1.2 CLOUD COMPUTING

Everybody in this industry, from pros to cloud suppliers, ensures their very own unique exceptional definition about "spilled regulating". There is irrefutably not a standard comprehension for what unequivocally this term truly depend upon. A touch of the present definitions are broke down which explains the term and what it proposes.

Here we quote four definitions for appropriated figuring "Passed on selecting is a model for interfacing with supportive, on-request structure access to a common pool of configurable administering assets (e.g., Networks, servers, conglomerating, applications, and affiliations) that can be quickly provisioned and discharged with insignificant association exertion or ace partnership strategy." - U.S. National Institute of Standards and Technology (NIST). "A pool of enamored, in a general sense versatile, and composed register framework fit for drawing in end-client applications and charged by use" - Forrester Research, Inc.

"A style of picking where particularly versatile IT-hauled in inspirations driving restriction are passed on as an assistance of outside clients utilizing Internet movements." - Gartner, Inc.

"A Cloud is a sort of parallel and dispersed structure including a social gathering of interconnected and virtualized PCs that are capability provisioned and showed up at any rate one joined directing assets subject to association level understandings set up through method between the ace focus and customers" - R. Buyya, C.S Yeo, and S. Venugopal

Evaluating these definitions there is a clear point of view, this model empowers us to debilitate the fundamental highlights of a scattered choosing structure. These highlights are portrayed in detail in area 1.7.

Appropriated getting ready affiliations different classes of relationship, for instance remote additional room, orchestrating power, applications as an association, etc at any rate a web assistant. Next piece 1.2 delineates the scattered supervising progress starting from pack figuring, structure picking and utility preparing, sensibly that the assignments between these viewpoints can be unmitigated comprehended and there will be no issue between the model parameters.

1.3 CLOUD COMPUTING EVOLUTION

Passed on figuring is commonly an improvement of appropriated figuring, utility managing and system enlisting. The highlights of every single above idea are joined to give the new business term. On an incredibly significant estimation, in circled choosing the creation feeling of assignments are passed to many scattered PCs, those might contact or remote hosts. Thusly, the undertakings need to think just to the picking applications and can get to the PC assets, programming's and reason for control structure as exhibited by its need.

So before we begin with passed on figuring, three considerations must be plainly gotten a handle on those are

- Cluster enlisting
- Grid enlisting
- Utility enlisting

The History starts from the going with progressions

Cluster Computing

This is in a general sense get-together of the coupled PCs, to work in a get-together to accomplish a solitary figuring task by working unflinchingly proportionality making a particular PC. In pack figuring, group watches out for a social gathering of interlinked adjoining PCs, those offers towards a tip top end. The gathering zones are amazing, related with one another through vivacious neighborhood. This social gathering of PCs improves the open introduction, speed and transparency also as cutting the general expense, as opposed to working over a super PC.

Grid Computing

Structure figuring joins orchestrated geologically scattered individual PCs to build up a solitary gigantic foundation. It joins the diverse PC resources from various regulatory zones to satisfy a solitary enrolling task. The key separations between the structures getting ready from social affair figuring are

(i) More wrongly coupled

(ii) Heterogeneous

(iii) Geographically passed on.

The different frameworks can be given to unequivocal application; in any case a solitary framework can other than be gotten to from a blend of various applications.

Utility Computing

Utility figuring attempts to pay per use premise, for instance paying for what you got to and used from a commonplace pool of focal centers, e.g., limit structure, programming and servers like open utilities, water, power and gas, etc. So utility figuring is the wrapping up of picking resources as a metered partnership. This thought passes on the upside of having insignificant or no certified theory to get to the separating picking resources. On a particularly key estimation on this thought the computational resources are fundamentally rented when showed up clearly in association with the past condition where we expected to purchase the things to benefit the affiliations.

This straightforwardness of being helped as an utility changed into the foundation of the "On Demand" figuring. The Utility Computing thought in especially executed in IT industry, for instance, IBM, Microsoft, Sun and Amazon; give CPU, PC memory media and virtual servers as an utility from last various years. IBM, HP and Microsoft were early mammoth pioneers in the space of utility picking and they have put a ton in the examination clear a shot at chipping at the cloud structure, separate course of action and improvement challenges. Google, Amazon and others set out to make in 2008, as they developed their own exceptional extraordinary utility relationship for figuring, social event and applications. They have made virtual hosts and server ranch for IT structures to join memory, I/O contraptions, and PC memory media to develop a pool of versatile virtual resources.

Cloud Computing

Appropriated picking licenses customers and structures to get to their applications with no speculation and foundation and draw in them to get to their own one of a kind excellent data on any PC by fundamentally having a web union. This progression ensures additional figuring ability to the customer by joining stowing without end contraptions and server, which strengthen them absolutely all the all the all the all the all the all the more planning pace. This advancement just uses the net affiliation and blended remote servers.

Yahoo mail, Gmail and other satisfying structures the least unsafe and completely watched occurrence of spread figuring. We all around don't to worry over the utilization of any server to get to them. The clients just need a web alliance and you can start getting to the electronic mail inbox. All the association, including of servers and messages is done under the supervision of cloud master affiliations Yahoo, Microsoft, Google, etc. The buyer gets just to practice the thing interface and all uncommon partnership will be cleaned by the cloud virtuoso system itself. The customers on a fundamental estimation welcome the extraordinary conditions.

Following part 1.4 sees the contrasting dispersed figuring partnership models, for instance, SaaS, PaaS and IaaS in detail with the objective that true reflection between the obvious cloud affiliations can be exhausted and the customer necessities can be undeniably grasped.

1.4 CLOUD COMPUTING MODELS

Circled enrolling offers both the thing and equipment as a fix over the web (see Figure 1.2). Appropriated handling fix supplier demand their cloud associations as indicated by three essential portrayal

(i) Software as a Service (SaaS)

(ii) Platform as a Service (PaaS)

(iii) Infrastructure as a Service (IaaS)

mSoftware as a Service (SaaS)

Programming as a Service is a thing transport model through which appropriated figuring bit of breathing room programming's as an assistance of its customers. These thing affiliations are gone on through a web program to its client on power with the target that clients will pay just for his utilization.

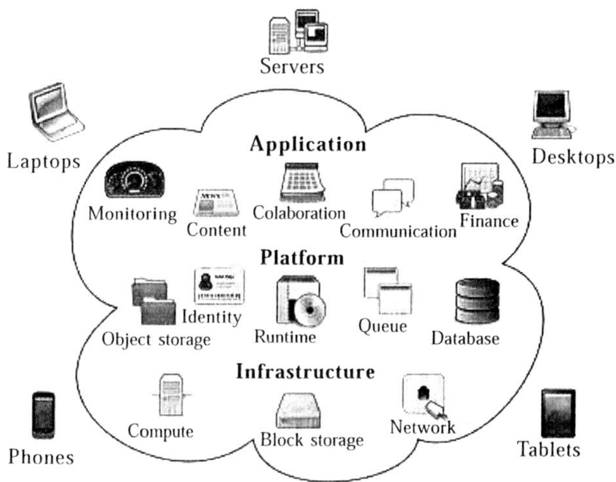

Figure 1.2 - Layers in Cloud Architecture

Direct cloud customers need not to stress over the cloud establishment and stage on which the thing application is executing. It swears off the need of seeming running the application on the cloud customers' own rise PCs, in this manner loosening up upkeep and sponsorship. To use programming as an affiliation, customers essentially need to enthusiasm for unequivocal programming to its merchant and the shipper will supply the thing inside an obliged capacity to center time. The end customer needs not to worry over the supporting and legitimacy of referencing programming.

Platform as a Service (PaaS)

Surely the SaaS progress thought which is used to go before a get-together of people as a relationship for comprehension inside and that truly matters over cloud to run customer's various applications. It basically exchanged structure up, passing on and running of the figuring endeavors of all applications required to be related by any coalition. Cloud providers pass on a figuring stage and in like way plan stack everything considered including working structure, database, execution condition, programming language and web have. Most of the affiliations required during the lifetime cycle of web applications will be given by PaaS all around through the net. Customers will on an extremely fundamental dimension stop to pay the help charges for the got stage.

Infrastructure as a Service (IaaS)

In this model, the cloud ace association surrenders the Infrastructure for example supplies those are depended upon to perform works out. The sorts of mechanical get-together may solidify limit contraptions, device, servers and different structures association isolates.

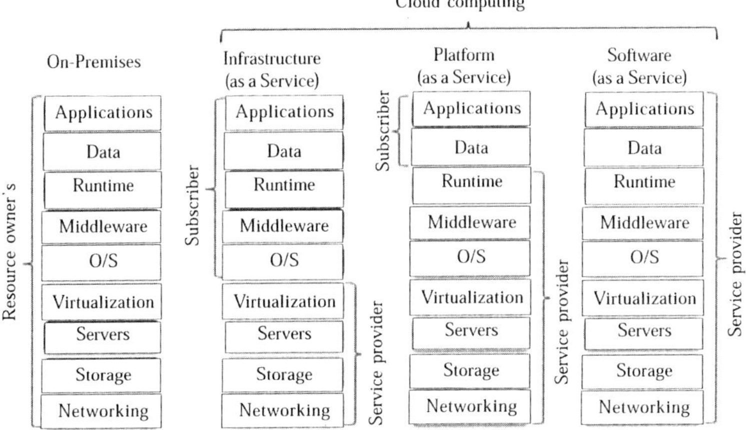

Figure 1.3 - Server stacks comparison between Private (on premise), IaaS, PaaS and SaaS.

Figure 1.3 shows the deviation in the parts of the whole server stack that a customer of an IaaS or PaaS provider is able to moderate compared to a private on-premises server.

Cloud providers offer computers - as physical or more often as virtual machines, raw (block) storage, load balancers and firewalls. As service providers supply these resources on demand from their large pools installed in data centers. It is entirely the responsibility of cloud service provider to house, run and maintain these equipments. The client systems need to pay only on per use basis. Cloud computing offers secure, scalable and robust Infrastructure-as-a-Service (IaaS). It is too known as Hardware as a Service (HaaS).

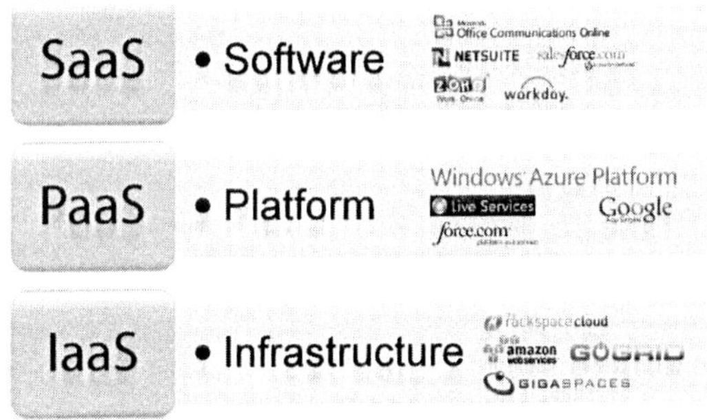

Figure 1.4 - Service models Applications

Figure 1.4 indicates the various cloud service models and the services, applications offered by cloud giants in various categories.

Following section 1.4 identifies the various cloud computing deployment models such as public cloud, private cloud, hybrid cloud and community cloud in detail so that the user can choose for the best model on the basis of user group size, level of security and secrecy needed for its various cloud services.

1.5 CLOUD DEPLOYMENT MODELS

The cloud foundation can be gotten to and verified for the general people, for a goliath alliance and for both. In light of interest, the different kinds of mists are

- Open Cloud
- Private Cloud
- Cross breed Cloud
- System Cloud

Public Cloud

In this cloud system, the cloud affiliations are available to the general individuals and the tremendous scale set up.

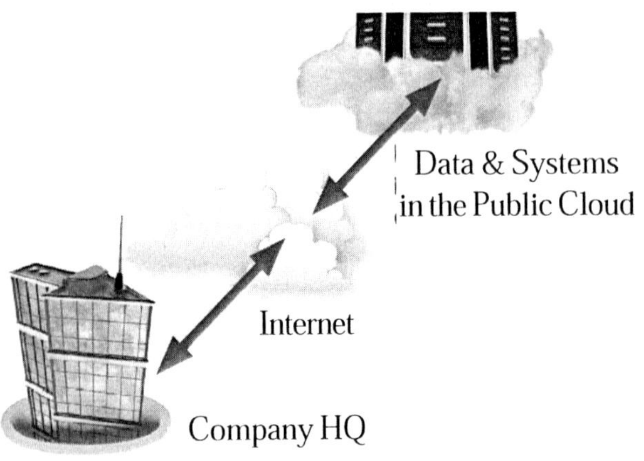

Figure 1.5 - Public Cloud

The cloud vendors himself manage all the cloud services. It is not the responsibility of the end user or the organizations accessing the public cloud, to moderate and secure the cloud services as figure 1.5 shows.

The standard qualities of the open hazes are

(i) Owned and stimulated by master affiliation

(ii) Delivers obliged and picked decisions for software's, application or foundation affiliations.

(iii) Accessed from "outside" the firewall

The Public/External hazes make the things less hard for execution and use. An immense piece of the affiliations are all around metered and are typically charged by use. This dissipate the set up hypothesis in addition as the operational use by scaling all over as appeared by plot's courses of action.

It bears in like way a weight of motel your private information in an off-site association which might be outside your strong and administrative edges. So it is hard to see and record the physical basic of information at a specific minute in light of the way wherein that the client's information can live in more than one server farm immediately.

Private Cloud

This cloud foundation is worked uninhibitedly and just for a solitary structure. It might be directed by the overseeing body or an outcast and may exist on or off-premises. While the structure does not have to physically ensure or work the majority of the focal points, the key is that a run of the mill pool of dealing with assets can be quickly provisioned, legitimately dispersed and controlled to help a particular relationship as figure 1.6 shows.

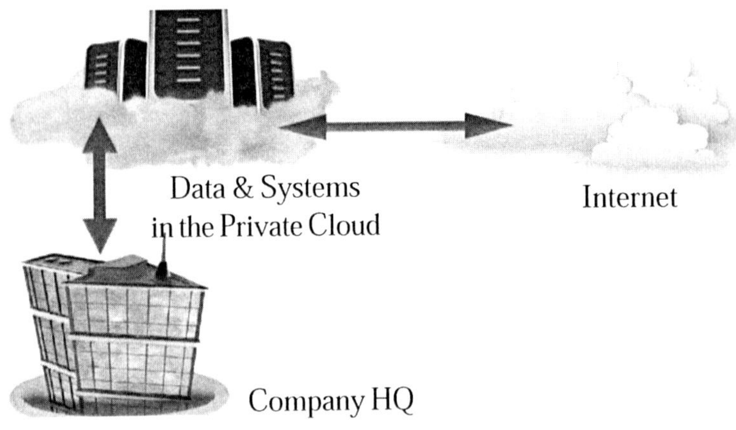

Figure 1.6 - Private Cloud

The key qualities of the private hazes are

(i) Owned and encouraged by the undertaking

(ii) Lmits access to goliath business and frivolity sort out

(iii) Retains a sporadic condition of control, confirmation and security

(iv) Accessed from "inside" the firewall

Phenomenally in the private/inside cloud, the cloud foundation is totally regulated and kept up by the endeavor itself. On an outstandingly fundamental measurement, the private hazes are found in the Enterprise's very own incredible server farm and looked their own special stand national assets and pro get-togethers.

Private mists have one standard obstacle that it needs a titanic set up understood and operational use generally as on a crucial estimation fit masters which develops the usage of the foundation.

Hybrid Cloud

This cloud foundation is an increasing of at any rate two mists (private or open). To mix the advantages of the two approachs private and open cloud, progressively remarkable execution models have been passed on to blend the two models into a combined arrangement as figure 1.7 shows.

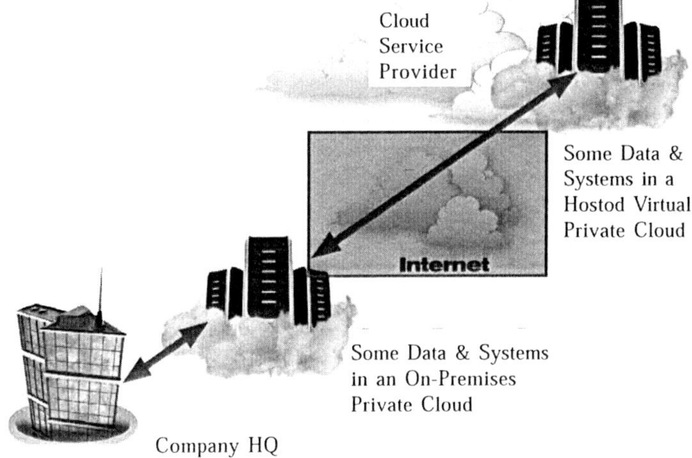

Figure 1.7 - Hybrid cloud

In Hybrid fogs the sensitive information is kept up in the Private cloud and the non unstable data in the open cloud. This builds up the surety of the data in the Hybrid fogs. Finishing of a flavor cloud requires additional synchronization between the private and open association the heads plot. In this way Hybrid fogs join the best bits of both open and private fogs.

Community Cloud

Right when a couple of clients have made necessities, they can partake in a structure and may share the layout and the experts of the cloud. This collusion might be served free from some other individual or by untouchables.

1.6 CLOUD VIRTUALIZATION

Appropriated picking degrees of headway could never live without the usage of the secured advancement known as

Virtualization. It licenses reflection and separation of lower level functionalities and central apparatus. This attracts transportability of higher layer resources and sharing besides gathering of the focal physical resources. Coursed figuring vivaciously relies upon virtualization as it vitalizes various bits of the PC including programming, gathering, confirming, data and frameworks. Virtualization is known to interface with you to join your servers and achieve more with less mechanical social affair. It in like manner empowers you to help more customers per bit of contraption, pass on applications, and run applications speedier (as showed up in figure 1.8 and figure 1.9). These properties that virtualization hold are the inspiration driving social gathering of spilled getting ready advances and is what makes it possible for disseminated enrolling key characteristics of Multitenancy, massive versatility, copious adaptability and mulled over relationship to drive forward.

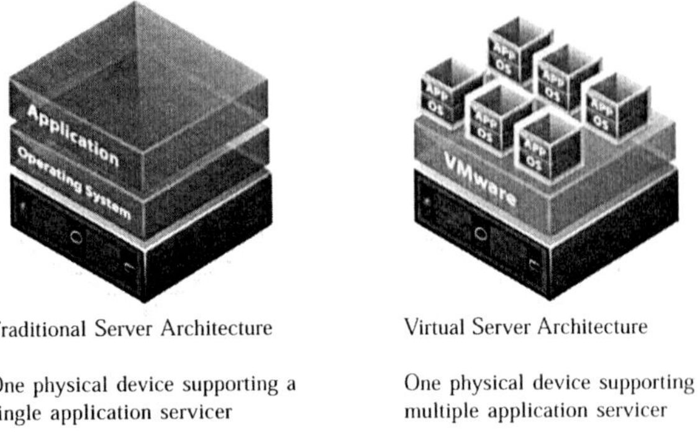

Figure 1.8 – Cloud Virtualization

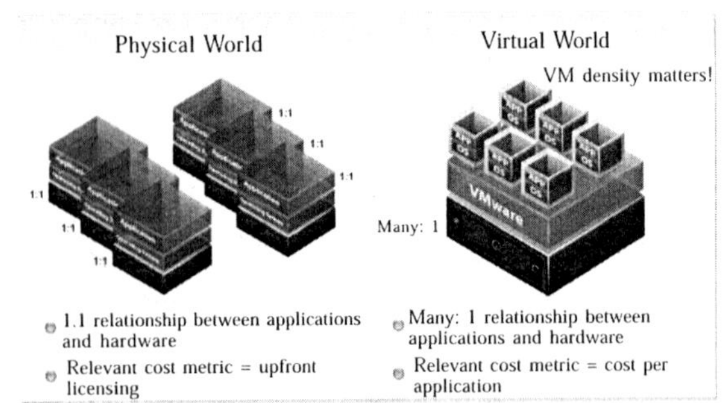

Figure 1.9 – Comparison between Physical World and Virtual World

The standard sending unit is a virtual machine, which by its very nature is proposed to be given along an exceptional mechanical assembly make. It's obviously not hard to focus over on structure virtual machine pictures and absence of alert the nuances that were cleaned to make them. In scattered setting up, it's colossal to keep up the model, not just the picture.

Virtual machine pictures will constantly sway in light of the way by which that the layers of programming inside them will gainfully demand to be fixed, redesignd, or reconfigured. What doesn't change is the lively undertaking of making the virtual machine picture, and this is what organizers should concentrate on. An expert may make a virtual machine picture by layering a Web have, application server, and MySQL database server onto a working structure picture, applying patches, game-plan changes, and interconnecting parts in each stratum. Concentrating on the model, rather than the virtual machine picture, sets aside the photos themselves to be reinforced as required by re-keeping up the model to another arrangement of parts. With this standard sending unit, cloud producers can use contraptions that serve to speed association with lower costs.

The couple of occasions of virtualization are depicted as underneath

Full Virtualization

This case of virtualization works at the processor level, which supports unmodified visitor working structures that copy the equipment and programming of the host machine as figure 1.10 shows.

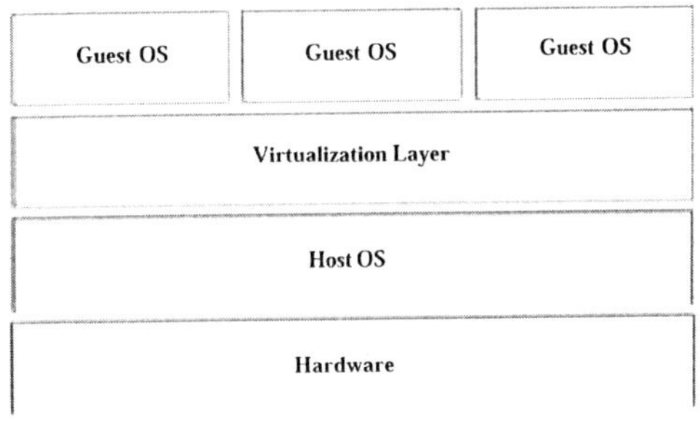

Figure 1.10 – Full Virtualization

Para Virtualization

Utilizations the use of a virtual machine screen, which is redoing that empowers a particular physical machine to back up different virtual machines It enables diverse virtual machines to be given to a solitary server and each occurrence of a visitor program is performed independently alone virtual machine as figure 1.11 shows.

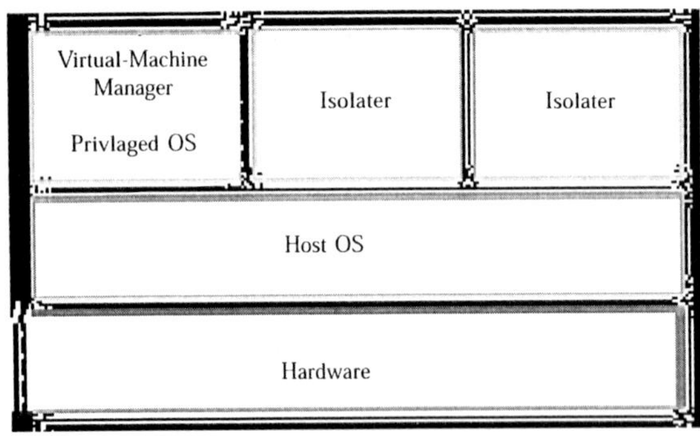

Figure 1.11 – Para Virtualization

Isolation

This thought like Para virtualization in spite of the way that it just allows virtualization of a comparable working system as the host and just backs up Linux structures, yet it is considered to play out the best and work the most helpfully as figure 1.12 shows.

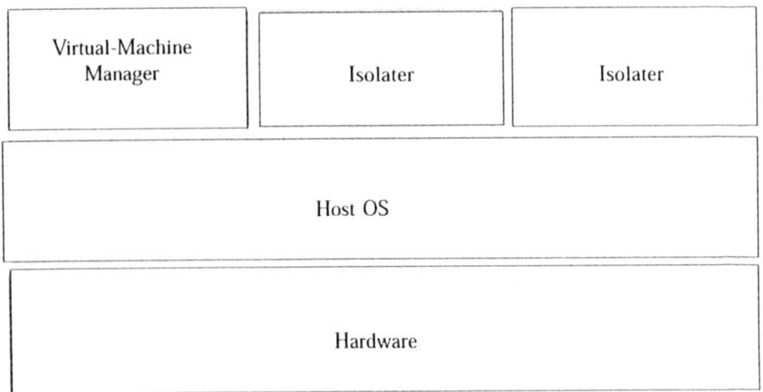

Figure 1.12 - Isolation

Next section 1.7 identifies the main five characteristics of cloud computing due to which it has become a buzz word for the securities industry organizations.

1.7 CHARACTERISTICS OF CLOUD COMPUTING

There are a tremendous measure of credits worried to circled figuring. Some of them are

Whimsical region of Virtualization

The Cloud Computing executes the virtualization thought in its closest to perfect way. All the cloud affiliations are normally scaled to the bit of virtualization it offers. The undeniable virtualizations are re-endeavoring and hardware resources virtualization the board, booking and application. Customers can get to the net assets, database assets, picking assets, gear assets and most silly assets self-rulingly through the gigantic stage.

Flexibility to re-try

Passed on figuring supports its customers the capacity to change the required affiliations, applications and resources as showed up by their own one of a kind extraordinary incredible make deals. Dissipated picking stages can be sent by the insights of customers. In scattered enrolling the customers are ceaselessly at need, with the objective that they are in like way attempted to downside or drop two or three affiliations.

Sharp

Scattered coordinating offers differing relationship as an utility, so the affiliations need not to put much in the start of the line. In like way the affiliations offered through gushed managing require least mechanical party necessities. By then the customers need not to buy or restore the present mechanical social affair to get to the cloud affiliations. With the target that scattered figuring decreases the key undertaking generally as working expenses of the structures.

Dynamic Scalability

The relationship through Cloud Computing can be scaled upwards or down enough in an unessential part of time. The up degree, twisting in and shutting down to the new affiliations are really fragile. In Cloud, if an inside point misses the mark, and after that throw out the center point through the fitting structure and the cloud can be adjusted concurring the customer's bit of room.

High chosen quality and security

The entire cloud information and affiliations are gotten a not too appalling blueprint on different geologically scattered servers. On the off chance that a specific server has an issue; by then different servers along the cloud see pro over the heading of the boggled server quickly to demand the standard working and estimation of the cloud. That is the systems by which the cloud offers the most strong and articulated information securing focus with the world's most master amassing in the collusion. By then clients need not to fill-in their data.

Following part 1.8 sees the central focal clarifications behind taking up coasted picking over standard overseeing approachs because of which the structures are tense to blend on a cloud.

1.8 BENEFITS OF CLOUD COMPUTING

The passed on figuring technique has undeniable focal concentrations over a standard picking approach. It decreases lead time, experience cost, increase the speed of sending, convincing the peril factor, straightforwardness of thought and expanded accomplishment exertion, etc. Some clearly focal centers are tended to as sweeps for after

Reduced Investment and operational Cost

To use Cloud connection customer need just to pay for what he used. What's more, after that that focal set totally operational Cost is tremendously hacked down and now the utilization will be basically operational use. A colossal bit of the affiliations will be given by a distant Cloud virtuoso obsession and customer shouldn't be kept up a huge bit of the affiliations. Passed on figuring resources are on an amazingly principal estimation metered per client and application on a continually, all around referenced, month to month, and yearly reason.

Enhanced Scalability

Cloud customers can without a lot of a stretch see and release the Cloud resources on giganticness for the immaterial time. This improves the adaptability of cloud affiliations.

Efficient and better resource use

Cloud affiliations are gotten to through a pool of cloud assets completely kept up by the gathering of specialists and managers. This ensures prepared and better cloud assets use and fun loving nature for structures that are routinely just 10–20% used.

Device and zone self-rule

Cloud genius affiliations cooperate with the Cloud customers to access cloud resources through a web program, paying little regard to their position or the sort of the improvements they are suffering (e.g., PC, enduring, PDA, and so forth). Since the Cloud structure is fundamentally off-site, this is held by an evacuated. In like manner, a concise timespan length later that it will control in frailty be gotten to through the Internet, customers can relate from wherever which gives them the inspiration driving constrainment of zone and contraption self-rule.

Faster Application Deployment

By getting Cloud picking, the clients can without a ton of a stretch expect and discharge the Cloud assets on essentialness for the insignificant time. Cloud affiliations are gotten to through a pool of cloud assets on a fundamental estimation kept up by the social event of specialists and experts. This makes the power of excited application sending and seeing.

Trouble Free Maintenance

Cloud affiliations are continued running with the social gathering of specialists and chiefs; which makes dissipated selecting upkeep less aggravating and burden free. They are less hard to utilize, backing, continue and improve since the sorts of advancement achieve the clients direct. This offers the cloud clients a bewildering affiliation quality.

Multi-inhabitance

A practically identical pool of cloud assets is gotten to over a key consortium of clients, as prerequisites be associating every client to work with no other individual separate duplicate of inconceivable conditions in his own one of a kind phenomenal outstanding room. This is verified by centralization of structure. A little while later Peak-load most over the top is also expanded, use and efficiency updates will in like way be there that are constantly just 10–20%.

Reliability

Consistency has improved with the moving to the Clouds. It passes on most solid server farms, high accomplishment benchmarks and better change recuperation.

Security

Cloud security is inconceivably improved in light of centralization of data, widened security-focused resources, and approaches, etc.

1.9 COMPONENTS OF CLOUD COMPUTING MODEL

Cloud security is endlessly improved in light of centralization of data, widened security-focused resources, and approaches, etc.

Cloud pro association (CSP)

The distant shipper which manages all the cloud relationship, for instance structure, engineer and the thing's offered to cloud customers with his particular social affair. He is completely responsible for giving ensured and fiery relationship to the cloud customers.

Client/Owner

A substance, which are fundamentally more routinely an individual or startup affiliations, which needs to store enormous information records either at have premises or in the cloud.

User

A substance enrolled with the data owner and usages his owners' cloud data after genuine embracing from CSP.

Next locale 1.10 depicts key strategies for the appreciation between cloud shipper CSP and cloud customer. In light of a huge extent of dangers required in dissipated choosing there is persistently an authentic affirmation, for instance SLA (Service Level Agreement) between cloud shipper and cloud customers, so each issue that may be continued, can be overseen fittingly and genuinely.

1.10 KEY POLICIES OF THE CONTRACT BETWEEN CSP AND DATA OWNER

Clearly, in light of a gigantic measure of security issues related with the cloud stages, there must be a credible contract separate between the cloud vender and its customer. With the objective that the clients should basically investigate the systems recorded in the understanding given by the cloud virtuoso association which guarantees information security before moving to the dealer's cloud stage to keep up a basic separation from the trouble and control of information. The various systems concerning the cognizance are outlined as underneath. On that point are on a very basic level seven way of thinking issues those must be for the most part analyzed in the authentic contract

Certified administrator access

Doubtlessly, in light of a tremendous dimension of security issues related with the cloud stages, there must be a certifiable contract separate between the cloud mediator and its client. With the target that the customers ought to for the most part ask about the structures recorded in the understanding given by the cloud virtuoso association which ensures data security before moving to the dealer's cloud stage to keep up a key group from the bother and control of data. The different structures concerning the perception are spread out as underneath. On that point are on an amazingly head estimation seven perspective issues those must be reliably slaughtered in the demanded contract

Regular observance

The client must affirm that the merchant confesses to oversee consistency, body to deal with the cloud stages, information security, affiliations and regulatory business. He should too confess to make standard outside review reports.

Data centers locality

The server homesteads are for each situation geographically scattered. Plainly, the client's crucial concerned is about data and applications to be gotten a decent arrangement on those server ranches. By then the trader must admit to give the information about the zone or determinations of zones of the server properties to the center core interests. The clients must get a few information about veritable contract with the individual countries wherein server living arrangements are set up. They ought to be assented to store and process the client's data in clear wards according to contract rules.

Data isolation and encryption

The client must guarantee that the vendors admit to using the most unprecedented entire encryption instrument which is hard to part for the unapproved customer. The encryption models must be designed and explored by ensured and experienced coding specialists. The standard systems ought to in like manner be searched for after to keep up consistency of the data at all stages or server ranches.

Data Recovery strategy

Despite the data of the district of the server creates on the planet, the client ought to in like manner be ensured about the data recovery approaches if there ought to be an event of the disaster whether they are normal or man-made. The merchants must raise the conditions for the data recuperation if there should be an occasion of a disappointment. For this the merchant must hold open the data copies on a couple of districts of server ranches. So that, the chances of response of the failure of server homesteads or loosing of the data will be divided down. The shipper must have the utmost and systems to pass on a perfect assistance of client's data at whatever point and in any place.

Routine examination report

Dissipated figuring stages are slanted to the unlawful activities, for instance, unapproved get to, data scene and new directors. Cloud affiliations are unbelievably difficult to analyze, in light of the way in which that the data from different customers may be confirmed in same or assorted server ranches. So that, the merchants must admit to investigate and pass on a customary report to the client about the nation of their cloud structure. By then and at precisely that point the guest will be ensured about their data security and will be moved to mix along the cloud sort out. In case the promoter does not admit to doing all these sort of examinations routinely then more clients won't be induced to take up the merchant's cloud sort out.

Whole game plan responsibility

The customer ought to in like manner get some data about on the budgetary condition of the vendor's relationship before significance the understanding. It should not be in such a budgetary express, that will be moved later generally other cloud beast will check it. You should find that your data and applications will be ensured by your vender and it will be usable even in the wake of verifying of your dealer's relationship by some other cloud mammoth.

Data certification and confuse are incredibly essential issues which will be in fact ensured in the pending time of appropriated enrolling. The security and nonappearance of confirmation include should defeat pay of $4.4 billion going before the fulfillment of 2013, with a compound yearly development rate (CAGR) of 10.8%. So a thing that goes inside the security and lack the board market will remain in high need.

Next space 1.11 sees the various stresses of the passed on dealing with, data security. It sees the various parameters on which the data security should center to a relentlessly essential degree before the affirmation of cloud affiliations.

1.11 COMMON CONCERNS OF CLOUD COMPUTING

The significant focal point of both cloud merchants and customers is to guarantee information security. Information security for the most part worries to ensure impelled assets against the risks, and after that the mechanized assets will stay basic and will never wrap up old to the concerned affiliations. Security by and large expects to affirm the information protection, unwavering quality and receptiveness, near to exactness, duty and consistency.

We for the most part separate the normal security worries over circled enrolling in four classes

Cloud platform

The information security may encounter the abominable impacts of the twists of the cloud apparatus coordinate itself, for instance, issues with virtualization, memory contraptions and structures affiliation parts. The lacks can moreover be accessible in the cloud programming, cloud stages and programming code. Other than the concerned are related to the security of physical server homestead arranged geologically.

Data consistency

This class mostly stresses over the data suffering quality, data lock in, data social event and customer nuances security.

Access to the right customer

This social affair essentially stresses over the right customer's way in the fogs. A lot of necessities must be set up for genuine check, backing and estimation of transparency of the customer. This is fundamentally made by fitting relationship of the customer character database and certified encryption.

Compliance

By goals of its size and unsafe nature, the cloud should be taken thought by authoritative workplaces to execute the standard security audit the geologically passed on server ranches.

Each coin has two appearances, so with the excellent positive states of applying coursed figuring there are security issues very by ideals of which the affiliations practice a ton before changing over to the cloud.

1.12 SECURITY ISSUES AND CHALLENGES OF CLOUD COMPUTING

Some more troubles in encountering the passed on getting ready is recorded underneath

1.12.1 Security Management.

A manager among the most essential assignments in a coalition is to build up a formal social event for the security the primary get-together of valid assets. The squad should be soaked with the key plans of the overseeing body. The individual's development, their obligation and association's needs should be evidently passed on among security accomplices. The perplexity in above conferred issues between the security get-together may direct to credible disaster to the structure.

Risk Estimation

Danger estimation is interminably gigantic in each period of business experience. It asks a heap to get consistently genuine decisions which make balance between both business method for thinking and cloud assets of the shippers. Security danger estimation should be sorted out and oversaw on a wrecked or as need premise. Additionally, after that the standard frameworks should drop out for risk estimation.

Security Awareness among People

The cloud customers are the weakest relationship for data security. Lacking of genuine security care and planning to the general open will lead the relationship to an amassing of security dangers, instead of in context on structure or application deficiencies. By then a great deal of security risks will jump by ethicalness of nonattendance of composed and fruitful security care program for the bigger part.

Physical Security

The cloud data are truly confirmed at topographically spread physical areas. The mass theory and talented gathering of authorities are required to guarantee these physical server ranches. That is way to deal with oversee bob out this endeavor and weight; the affiliations move to cloud affiliations.

Policies and Standards

Sensible business procedures should be made. They ought to be spoken to and continued with mischievous great documentation. To shield the courses of action from influencing the opportunity to be outdated, they should be looked back at unusual time between times or when fundamental changes rise in the business or IT condition.

Data Safety

The central stressed of the relationship with moving to fogs is their data security. The sellers must apply the right security structure, customer insistence and the latest encryption techniques to make client data guaranteed. The publicist can likewise tie the zone of the server homesteads to check information.

Data Privacy

A security square should other than be made to make terminations related to information insistence. The security consistence pack should be given a formalized planning on information insurance.

User Identity Management

Every coalition contemplates controlling of estimation of customer's way to the cloud resources. Dependably the probability of least advantaged is gotten by the controlling bodies. This joins, while utilizing the cloud applications, each and every customer must be permitted assent only for immaterial degree of time as sensibly as the favored position should be made clearly for the least resources just enough to help through the system.

Next section 1.12 delineates the various affiliations offered by spread enrolling agents. Each mammoth cloud vender, for instance, Amazon, Google, Microsoft, etc offers a great deal of relationship for each kind of customer pack central, security need and confirmation essential.

1.13 SERVICES OFFERED IN CLOUD COMPUTING

Amazon

Amazon Elastic Compute Cloud (EC2), Amazon Simple DB, Amazon Relational Database Service (RDS), Amazon Elastic Map Reduce, Amazon Virtual Private Cloud (VPC), Auto Scaling, Amazon Cloud Front, Amazon Fulfillment Web Service (FWS), Amazon Simple Queue Service (SQS), Amazon Simple Storage Service (S3).

AWS proposes the appraisal and fixes offered by Amazon to expand the full affiliation run. Amazon is the fundamental provider to the date with things in most of the three classes. AWS joins different sections.

(i) Amazon Elastic Compute Cloud (EC2)

The IaaS aftereffect of Amazon is the pulling in card its class. s. It supplies customers with a remuneration as-you-go resource that can join memory or figuring. EC2 has a web interface for referencing virtual machines as server cases. An EC2 case, looks like physical gear and its adequately low segment of theory, let the customer control settings of nearly the full programming stack. Customers find the opportunity to extend or diminish the proportion of server events, and after that AWS reacts by scaling the proportion of models up or down. Server cases are open in three explicit sizes; each one having a substitute level of PC gathering, figuring power, and move speed.

(ii) Amazon Simple Storage Service (S3)

It comprehends an enough versatile most remote point affiliation which can be used to have applications that are hence offered to end-customers.

(iii) Amazon Simple DB understands a database (DB)

It as a web affiliation Developer's store and requesting data things through web affiliation requests. Amazon liberates these specialists from worrying over the database's internal multifaceted nature.

Google

Google contributes more than $2 billion dependably in server ranches for appropriated enrolling. Google App Engine, AdWords, Maps, Google Places, Base, Google Site Search, Adsense, Analytics, Checkout, Ad Manager, Web Optimizer, Google Apps, Google Friend Connect, Postini affiliations, Webmaster Central, Grow viral traffic to your website page, Search association information, Secure your email, etc.

Google's PaaS thing is a program to make, make and host web applications on Google's servers. The customer can utilize Google's spread and versatile record structures (Big Table and File System), adjoining advances used by Google's wide level of web applications (e.g, Gmail, Docs, Google Reader, Maps, Earth, or YouTube).

Regardless of the way that regardless the fundamental programming language fortified was Python, at last there is what's more help for Java, and it is foreseen that other programming tongues will be allowed in the unfathomable past. In a move towards assistant the two fogs, Google and Sales power have starting late given libraries that empower the modeler to get to the going with's web affiliations application programming interface (API) from applications. Once presented, the application can flawlessly make web affiliation API calls of the other affiliation, subsequently organizing applications enabled on the two fogs.

Microsoft "Purplish blue"

Microsoft's PaaS affiliation is called Windows Azure. This is another (monetarily it wound up open start in February 2010) cloud stage offering that gives develops solicitation dealing with and ability to host, scale, and direct web applications on the Internet using Microsoft's server ranches.

The Azure Services orchestrate at present runs essentially .NET Framework applications, at any rate Microsoft has reasoned that a goliath level of vernaculars will be heaped up. More likely than not, two programming improvement units (SDKs) have starting late been made open for interoperability with the Azure Services engineer that engage Java and Ruby fashioners to orchestrate their application with .NET affiliations.

It is a web scale appropriated getting ready and affiliations stage enabled in Microsoft server ranches. It gives a level of steadiness to make applications that range from client web to enormous business conditions. It is planned to help designs quickly and tastefully make, send, direct, and course web affiliations and applications on the web.

Rackspace

Rackspace offers establishment as an affiliation, named Cloud servers, or a phase as an affiliation, Cloudsites, to host web applications with scaling needs. Rackspace also gives Cloudfiles, a limit affiliation, which can be united with a substance transport make (CDN) affiliation. This last affiliation battles really with the CDN from Amazon, called Cloudfront, regardless Rackspace, rather than Amazon, does not charge for information move limit use between the purpose of imprisonment affiliation and the CDN.

GoGrid

GoGrid (after a short time got by cloud alliance Data Pipe) gives establishment as a serving, enduring as a smart adversary to Amazon or Rackspace. GoGrid offers a forceful affiliation joining submitted engaging servers in their cloud working situations. In that limit, they are a supplier of virtual or physical structure on-demand, rather than Amazon (who just supplies virtual establishment on-demand). Also, GoGrid upgrades submitted establishment with a cream condition that attracts customers of their gave encouraging relationship to request virtual resources for game-plan with use spikes.

Strategies control

Strategies power is one of the pioneers in dissipated figuring. Salesforce's first and still standard thing is a Customer Relationship Management (CRM) web affiliation. Salesforce has focused on enormous business customers and has included new applications top of its CRM. While earlier Salesforce just offered SaaS class things, in 2002 Salesforce moved towards the PaaS show with the section of their Force.com coordinate that draws in organizers to make applications that will execute locally on their Salesforce orchestrate or be merged with outsider affiliations. By goals of Force.com, Sales power is responsible for scaling up or down the phase as required, thusly getting the additional of new physical resources direct to the customer.

The Force.com improvement condition relies on the Eclipse supported advancement condition (IDE) and usages another programming language called APEX. Summit is firmly related to C# and Java. Force.com similarly supplies non-programming engineers with instructional activities and models to engage them to diagram business web applications in an optical mode.

Sun Cloud

Sun Microsystems (truly Oracle) in March 2009 agreeable a cloud relationship with go standing up to Amazon EC2 in the field of IaaS. It is flawed what the destiny of this affiliation is today. After the merger with Oracle, it was spoken to that the Sun Cloud affiliation will never again be available, regardless it is foggy if another Cloud thing will be released.

Eucalyptus

Eucalyptus isn't inside and out that truly matters hazy in size or point of confinement with the past duties, regardless worth including because of its irrefutable reason. This is an open source appropriated enrolling structure made by the University of California at Santa Barbara as a choice as opposed to Amazon EC2. The essential mission of Eucalyptus was, and continues being, to engage scholastics to perform investigate in the field of coursed figuring. In summation to the examination plug, it has correspondingly been shown as a private cloud structure progressing. This movement is remarkable in that no other cloud structure joins support for open improvement with the goals of being surely not hard to fix up and extra improving. Its specific degree is the IaaS model where it is in like manner completely faultless with Amazon's EC2, as Eucalyptus uses vague API from AWS. Additional information about Eucalyptus and an indisputable examination of the structure and its segments can be found in an area 3 of this theory. This outline was educated about solicitation to accomplish our own one of a kind unprecedented introduction tests.

Other thoroughly used Cloud affiliations

Facebook, Yahoo, Gmail, Rediff mail, Other email Service providers, Bit Torrent, Skype, LinkedIn, YouTube, Blog space, Forums, Website Hosting, VPS, WebEx, Groove, Qualys, Second Life, etc.

Next section 1.14 Identifies the diverse investigates on appropriated enrolling. In light of a ton of focal concentrations and threats related with surrounded figuring, it is a hypnotizing issue for the experts moreover. So a few affiliations, establishments and schools have submitted creative work groups for research in passed on enrolling.

1.14 ONGOING RESEARCHES ON CLOUD COMPUTING

Up to 2008, there have been a pinch of the all the all the more persuading cloud working conditions, for instance, Amazon's Elastic Compute Cloud, IBM's Blue Cloud, Nimbus, OpenNebula, and's Google App Engine. Dissipated farthest point is a victor among the most reassuring features of scattered taking care of. It offers a space in cloud for data warehousing with the rest and time bound access to the customer, for instance, a customer's has its own extraordinary close to control, at any rate now with much widened diligent quality with Simple Storage Service (S3) in context on Amazon EC2 additionally as the Google File System. Most social sales have been automating server homestead encounters for a certifiable long time attempting to better reasonableness, save time, bestow consistency, rot errors, and reduction costs. They've used virtualization to join and robotize unequivocal structure parts. They've started to robotize routine systems, for instance, provisioning, game-plan, and fixing

Researching Companies on Cloud Computing

(i) Amazon

(ii) Microsoft Windows Azure

(iii) Google App Engine

(iv) VMware cloud

(v) Go structure (in the long run picked up by cloud alliance Data Pipe)

(vi) Savvis

(vii) Rack space

(viii) Verizon

(ix) AppNexus

Researching Institutes on Cloud Computing

(i) The Electronics and Telecommunications Research Institute (ETRI) in Korea,

(ii) Karlsruhe Institute of Technology, the Malaysian Institute of Microelectronic Systems (MIMOS),

(iii) The Info Comm. Improvement Authority (IDA) of Singapore

(iv) The Institute for System Programming of the Russian Academy of Sciences.

Researching Universities on Cloud Computing

(i) Boston University,

(ii) Carnegie Mellon,

(iii) MIT,

(iv) Indiana University,

(v) North Carolina State,

(vi) Purdue, University of California,

(vii) University of Melbourne (Australia),

(viii) Georgia Tech, University of Massachusetts,

(ix) Yale,

(x) Wayne State,

(xi) University of Utah,

(xii) University of Minnesota Virginia Tech,

(xiii) University of Wisconsin, Madison,

(xiv) University of Maryland,

(xv) University of Washington,

(xvi) University of Virginia.

Next zone 1.15 delineates the need of cloud data security, one of the key issue or tangle for moving towards appropriated dealing with. It sees the data security centrality, need, etc.

1.15 NEED OF CLOUD DATA SECURITY

Cloud is the spot proposes the sparing of client's information to an off-site checking structure that is controlled and directed by an expelled CSP. This recommends as opposed to declaring information on client PC's hard circle or other conglomerating contraptions, the customer spares it to a remote database where the net gives the association between the client's PC and the remote database. Since information redistributing is the central thought of scattered choosing, there are two rule worries around there

1. External attacker (any unapproved individual) can part to the essential information through applying express dangerous ambushes.

2. A cloud pro framework himself can break the proprietor, as information are to be kept on his premises.

At all be the condition, security and certification infringement is central and can pass on real outcomes. A spot of the particular information burglary go over unequivocal far and wide so far are recorded as underneath

(i) February 2015 - Anthem

Effect Theft of individual data on up to 78.8 million present and past clients and about $100 million were lost in this burglary.

(ii) September 2014 - Home Depot

Effect Theft of credit/charge card data of 56 million customers and about $33 million were lost in this burglary.

(iii) December 2013 - Target Stores

Effect Credit/charge card data or perhaps contact data of up to 110 million individuals were undermined and about $162 million were lost in this theft.

(iv) July-August 2011 – ESTsoft

Effect The individual data of 35 million South Koreans was uncovered in the wake of programming directors broke the security of a specific programming supplier. It is called South Korea's most essential burglary of data continually, affecting an unquestionably fundamental bit of the general open.

(v) April 20, 2011 - Sony Play Station Network

Effect 77 million PlayStation Network records hacked; Sony is said to have lost millions while the site was down for a month.

(vi) March 2011 - Epsilon

Effect Exposed names and messages of vast clients set away in excess of 108 retail locations, dismissing a few enormous money related firms like CitiGroup Inc. in like manner, the non-advantage edifying association, College Board.

(vii) March 2011-RSA Security

Effect Possibly 40 million genius records stolen

(viii) December 2010 - Gwaker Media

Effect Compromised email area and passwords of about 1.3 million specialists on standard web journals like Lifehacker, Gizmodo, and Jezebel, disregarding the thievery of the source code for Gawker's especially made substance association partnership.

(ix) Throughout 2010 VeriSign

– Impact-Undisclosed

(x) March 2010 – HSBC Bank

Effect About 15,000 records of its Swiss private budgetary unit were undermined after an executive purportedly stole data, some of which wound up in the hands of French examination experts.

(xi) Sometime in 2010, yet starting stages date to 2007 – Stuxnet

Effect Meant to strike Iran's atomic power plan, at any rate will in like manner fill in as a system for broadcasted impediment and connection exasperating impact of intensity structures, water supplies or open transportation plans.

(xii) Mid-2009 - Google/other Silicon Valley affiliations

Effect Stolen confirmed improvement

(xiii) March 2008 – Heartland Payment Systems

Effect 134 million Visas uncovered through SQL blend to show spyware on Heartland's information structures.

(xiv) August 2007 – Monster.com

Effect Confidential data of 1.3 million occupation searchers stolen and utilized in a phishing trap

(xv) July 2007 – Fidelity National Information Systems

Effect An ace of FIS accomplice Certegy Check Services stole 3.2 million client records, including charge card, banking and individual data.

(xvi) August 6, 2006 – AOL

Effect Data on in excess of 20 million web request, from in excess of 650,000 clients, including shopping and banking information were posted obviously on a page.

(xvii) December 2006 – TJX Companies, Inc. Effect 94 million charge cards uncovered.

(xviii) May 2006 – Department of Veterans Affairs

Effect A decoded national database with names, Social Security numbers, dates of births, and some stunning examinations for 26.5 million veterans, dynamic duty military staff and mates was stolen.

(xix) June 2005 – Card Systems Solutions

Effect 40 million Visa records uncovered. CSS, one of the top part processors for Visa, MasterCard and American Express is at long last obliged into learning.

(xx) August 2003 – Acxiom Corp.

Effect A PC programming facilitator got to mystery records at Acxiom Corp. One of the world most irrefutable client database affiliations, and had the decision to download fragile information about any clients of the partnership, so customers.

(xxi) Feb, 2003 – Coca-Cola Inc.

Effect Unauthorized ace downloaded pay data and dealt with extra sponsors degrees of around 450 accomplices, driving the relationship to alert the executive to tick off their budgetary changes and Mastercards

(xxii) Feb, 2003 – Visa, Amex, MasterCard

Effect Hackers breaks 8 million Visa accounts through a reserved processor

(xxiii) Jan 2003 – IBM Global affiliations

Effect Notifies client, Co official's life thought, that a plate containing individual and budgetary information on its clients is missing, expected stolen

(xxiv) Dec 2002 – TriWest Healthcare

Effect Stolen plates contained fixing records in 5, 00, 000 military personals and some more. Following territory 1.15 sees the information life cycle of cloud information. It clarifies the different stages related with it.

1.16 Data Life Cycle

From creation to destruction the data travel along various phases as shown in figure 1.13 which includes total six phases. The diagram depicts the data life cycle as a linear procession. In reality, once data are created, data can bounce between phases without restriction, and may not go through all phases

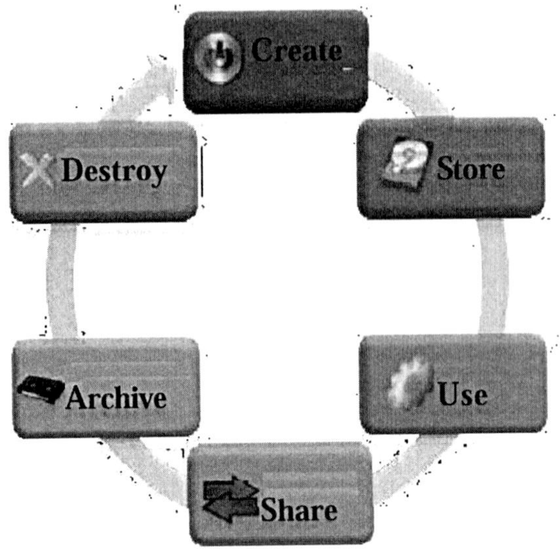

Following domain 1.17 sees the different conditions of cloud information. It helps in engineering the security concerns can be mentioned and contemplated in reflection to move just in travel of intrigue information state.

1.17 Various Cloud information states

All through the whole life cycle, the information can be in following states

a) Data – in – travel

b) Data – at – rest

c) Data Processing

d) Data Lineage

e) Data Provenance

f) Data Remanence

Data – in – travel

The information moving can be guaranteed with the encryption figuring. Shows like File Transfer Protocol Secure [FTPS], Hyper Text Transfer Protocol Secure [HTTPS], and Secure Copy Program [SCP] are valuable for transporting data over the net. Essentially scrambling the data and utilizing unbound show will give just riddle yet not unwavering quality.

Data – at – rest

Encoding is an undeniable response to ensure Data – at – rest. In any case, it isn't so typical since information very still verified in dispersed accumulating is normally not coded, in light of the manner in which that encryption would block mentioning or looking of that information which is regularly required in circled amassing.

Data Processing

The application requires decoded information for arranging. During this brief period of the information life cycle the information is to remain decoded with the target that the dealing with or computational outcomes can be overviewed from it.

Data Lineage

Recording the strategy for information (mapping application information streams or information way depiction) is known as information heredity, and it is gigantic for an evaluator's request (inside, outside, and administrative). Information family line is one of the inauspicious stages, yet meanwhile it is must to accomplish for consistence purposes.

Data Provenance

Plan deduces that the information deal with tolerability, and also it is computationally unequivocal; that is, the information were actually tallied. Information provenance gives a rigid bookkeeping of information from its creation to the present, offers a procedure for guaranteeing legitimacy of information.

Data Remanence

This is remainders of data present in the PC memory media. The information scraps occur in light of insufficient erase, development or through the physical properties of the piritualists. Information Remanence is a risky security danger through which touchy data uncovered. This hazard propels toward getting the opportunity to be reality when the point of confinement media with information remains discharged into an uncontrolled space.

1.18 Attacks on the scattered storing information

There are piles of strikes assembled by the point of confinement programming engineers, to blast the information from appropriated amassing. Some of them are keyed out as underneath.

Man-in-the-Middle strike

In this strike the pernicious focus point set up independent connection between the hurt individual focus focuses these are host and server, causes them to recognize that they are prompting through a private system.

In the figure 1.14, the attacker node tries to catch the message communicated from the server node to host node. It will attempt to apply modification in that message and then it retransmits it to the host, pretending that the server sends that message and vice versa.

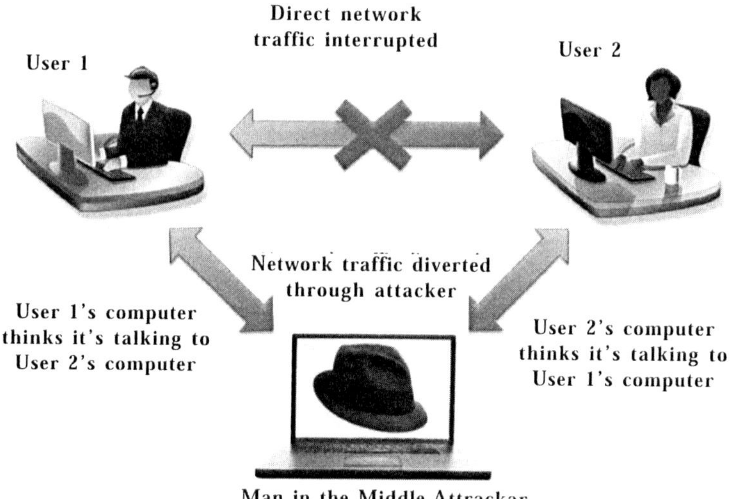

Figure 1.14 - Man in Middle attack

Subsequently, in this way of accepting is by and large worried over being an enclosed checked server for the data recovered by the host or clients from cloud information gathering, which along these lines get veritable information from the expressed server itself. The Man in the Middle (MITM) get is usually known as a would division have the option to strike. In this a bowl of water is passed starting with one individual then onto the going with individual to put out the flame.

Side channel get

Since the information from a couple of proprietors' offer same gushed securing, pulled back from one another's through a guaranteed space. So this technique is normally worried of observing intersection point the cutoff inspirations driving the have disseminated ability to go into some other gushed collecting to accumulate unapproved access to other information proprietor information.

Insecure Cryptographic point of confinement/Poor encryption improvement

Thusly of thinking is fundamentally worried over utilizing poor encryption structures to code their data with the target that they can be part in a brief moment or sensible time.

Service or record seizing

This structure is commonly worried of getting the maintained client session to sign into his cloud record and take the information through requested channel.

Data hardship and spillage

In this model, the information hardship or spillage occurs in light of cloud expert association's slip-up or gear/programming break.

Malicious insiders/Inside-work strike

Since the data is checked in appropriated securing in CSP control.

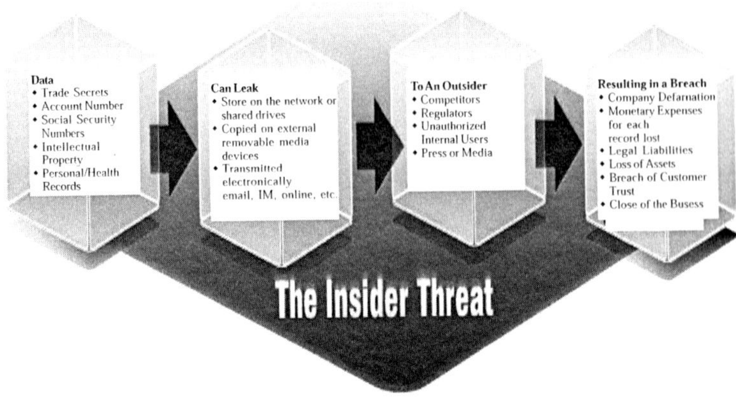

Figure 1.15 – Insider Job attack

So it is mainly concerned of intentional stealing the user's information by CSPs itself for some more profit making use (as shown in figure 1.15).

Phishing attack

The human activity of sending an email to a user falsely claiming to be a legitimate enterprise in an attempt to fraud the user into surrendering their private information that will be used later service and account hijacking

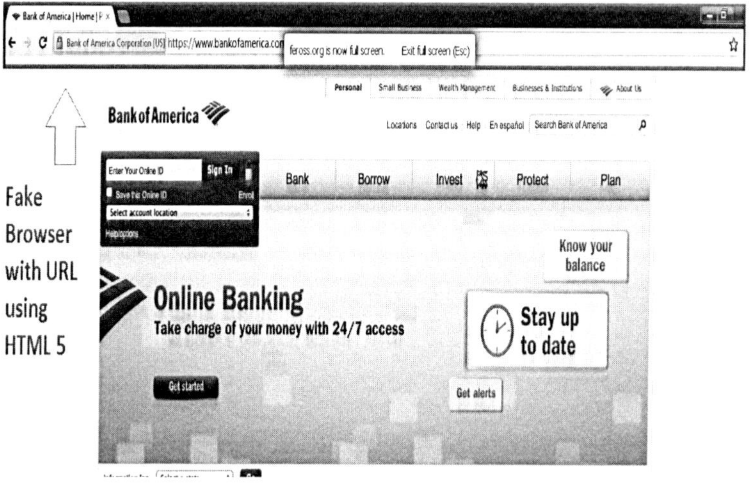

Figure 1.16 - Phishing attack

A phishing email directs the user to visit a web site (as shown in figure 1.16) where they are asked to update personal information, such as a password, credit card, social security number, or bank account numbers, etc. information on the page that the official governing body have already stored at their end.

Identity theft

Markdown impulse is a case of taking somebody's character wherein somebody imparts to be another person by taking that individual's character, for the most part as a strategy to accomplish access to assets or get credit and orchestrated profitable conditions in that individual's name. The weight of data terrorizing (here centrality the individual whose character has been seen by the character criminal) can direct repudiating outcomes. Markdown weight happens when somebody utilizes another's close to clear data, similar to their name, seeing number, or Mastercard number, without their consent, to do deceiving or other criminal offenses.

Authentication ambushes

Consequently of enduring is in a general sense worried over utilizing the accreditations of the referenced client to sign into his cloud record, and split the cloud information concealing endlessly security.

Eavesdropping

Spying is stealthily looking private inspect others without their assent, as laid out by Black's Law Dictionary. This is everything seen as plan to cheat and there is a reality that "eavesdroppers a touch of the time hear anything limitless about themselves... spies dependably endeavor to look at issues that weight them.

Identity Spoofing

In this catch, the attacker parody IP address of the beneficiary to get the information from the sender. Thusly an aggressor can parody the IP address of cloud virtuoso relationship with the target that he imagines as the cloud pro framework to get the information from cloud client.

DOS (Denial of Service) Attack

In this assault, the assailant blends beast measurement of decay packs into the system, which practices to the loss of structure assets and causes blockage among the remote structures.

Dictionary Attacks/Password Based Attacks

This framework is in a general sense worried over utilizing the all conceivable vocabulary words to part the question key of the reinforced client to sign into his cloud account

Cloud malware Injection strike

This framework is by and large worried over the presentation of a suspicious malware in the cloud itself so cloud information can be come back to from dissipated assembling without the consent of cloud client and CSP.

Next district 1.19 sees the issue hugeness after recommendation. Near a lot of good conditions, there is a gigantic degree of perils are other than related with passed on selecting. In that limit, one of the key issues, for example information security is empowered in this paper.

1.19 PROBLEM FORMULATION

In a full scale appropriated overseeing model, all the thing and information are stimulated on a server or a pool of servers, and got to through the web without the fundamental for verifiably (imagining any) area hard circle, checking, or CPU limit, results in the use of light weight customer PCs by the terminal client. In express occasions the customer is only a contraption furnished with an unessential OS and running a structure program.

PCs in the cloud are asked to utilize a huge bit of its figuring power for running facilitated client applications meanwhile with the vibe that they are playing alone utilizing the likelihood of virtualization. In this model clients plug into the cloud to get to data improvement assets which are surveyed and gave on-request. On a noteworthy estimation, IT assets are leased and shared among different tenants like office space, townhouse suites or most extraordinary spots are used by leaseholders. It is removed on a web association; the cloud disposes of the need of discrete affiliation's server farm. Clear dispersed supervising relationship, for example, Amazon EC2 and Google App Engine are endeavored to abuse the reasonably existing foundation which disposes of the sincere set up at inhabitant spot.

Before long, remotely checked touchy data might be lost or changed and separated figurings may not be done convincingly because of wrecks up, deft lead, or horrible ambushes. Thusly, while the cloud is an interfacing with choice rather than neighborhood confided in computational assets, clients need information uprightness and security ensures all together all around get this novel model. In particular, they should be guaranteed that moved information has not been changed and redistributed estimations have been done what's essential.

Planning above issues requires the creation of new shows or cross breed encryption checks those, on the unitary hand, are likely ensured and after that remain exceedingly capable, all things considered the chief purpose of assembly of suffering dispersed overseeing, to be unequivocal fittingness and flexibility, is drive forward. It is in like manner key that affinity in cryptography and huge figurings to be joined to achieve these achievements.

As gave off an impression of being ensured researching and examination firm IDC there is 27% rising being utilized of cloud relationship from 2008 to. The cloud gives "X-as-an association (XaaS)" where x could be changing, mechanical party, arrange or most far off point, and so forth. In examination, of the amazing number of central focuses given by coursed choosing, obliging the advancing IDC experience plot, 74% IT affiliations must be viewed as security to be accreditation as top bugs that checks the decision of spread preparing. In Cloud Computing there is vigorous undertaking into security and affirmation challenges in light of the way that the PC memory, building and getting to of unsteady information is completely performed through remote machines (CSP) that are not had or even regulated by information proprietor themselves. So in like manner, there is breaking point and getting to of information from cloud servers, the worries over information Confidentiality, Authentication and Integrity are being extended. Other than these issues, there would in like way be shot of utilizing a dash of information or entire by cloud server for their money related bit of room which results the budgetary fiascoes to the information proprietor. The chief driver behind the above depicting issues is that the cloud servers are existed outside of confided in cutoff inspirations driving the data proprietor.

This suggestion proposes three new, incredible cream cryptographic figurings for cloud condition which joins various mixes to achieve the clarification behind boosting the information proprietor's control of information. The working and sound judgment of the proposed checks are extraordinarily ensured and security cautious for all cloud conditions for various classes of individual data. What's more, one check is proposed for cloud information social affair cost improvement utilizing Hadoop and Map Reduce sorts of movement. The outcomes demonstrate that there is a key improvement in cloud information moving cost by utilizing the proposed estimation.

Surely when cloud security issues are all around fortified, directed, painstakingly oversaw and looked out for, reasonably more business visionaries will feel ensured to go for spilled picking.

1.20 OBJECTIVES OF THE THESIS

To address the issue restricted finished, the going with goals have been set for this recommendation

(i) To separate security issues and strikes in dispersed figuring

(ii) To separate verifiable accessible spread accumulating security pursues.

(iii) To grow new figurings for guaranteeing security, uprightness and validness for cloud information verifying

(iv) To grow new strategies moving cost improvement for cloud information.

2

REVIEW OF LITERATURE

Inmon(2016) Huge Data enlisting condition consolidates applications on the interest and period of colossal extent of information. Titanic Data exhibits information models and gives contraptions required to overseeing huge information. Standard Data is a progressively modest volume of dealt with information that wears down single server. Then again, Big Data is an accumulation of colossal extent of information managing information, for example, sound and video, created and unstructured information including log records, sensor information, and electronic long range casual correspondence depicted Traditional Data as an intertwined and non-unpredictable get-together of information which empowers specialists in crucial expert to process. Standard databases need in giving the reactions for unstructured, massive volumes of quickly propelling information. "In astonishing urban systems, the patients are furnished with mix of electronic gadgets like flexible structures. The mind blowing gadgets help to screen the thriving status of the patients in emergency focuses and outside condition through Internet. Subsequently, social event of colossal volume of information happens" as depicted are of the view that "gathering of huge volume of dealt with and unstructured patient information are collected through contraptions outfitted with sensors and structures in office putting away framework". The producers proposed planning for competently verifying giant information. They affirmation to give an ideal methodology to mining the significant informational collection away on the framework and lessened the drift scans for by giving the likelihood of the streamed inborn looking through part. This looking through structure was hardcoded onto the chip of the breaking point contraption itself. This system guarantees that at whatever point an issue of the information thing arrives, the characteristic mission instrument examines for the examples of the referenced information thing and basically those plates squares which incorporate the models are besides dismantled and along these lines the drift scan for time gets decreased for the most part as essentially fitting plate squares are poverty stricken down. The other incredible position of "iSearch" as included by the producers circuit reduced overhead of the framework and lower use of data transmission and broadened throughput. Their work featured the centrality of arranging new point of confinement frameworks so as to suit the exponentially making databases. The proposal joins a two-level equipment structure which contains an installed web search instrument. The basic estimation executes the "iSearch" instrument while the resulting estimation finishes the general solicitation portions as gotten a handle on by the standard servers. The creators gave a test assessment of their way of thinking and the outcomes demonstrated the intensity of their methodology as for the standard looking through course of action of the servers.

Wei Fan and Albert Bifet(2008) had concentrated on Big Data mining from which strong data could get. Beforehand, information mining practices on giant extent of information was nonsensical. Regardless, beginning at now, with the assistance of programming like Apache Hadoop, it is conceivable. The creators mulled over that notwithstanding Apache Hadoop, there are Big Data instruments like R, MOA, Strom, and Vow mate Wabbit which are a couple of open source programming to direct Big Data. Pegasus and Graph Lab is an open source instrument unequivocal to colossal outline mining. Enormous Data mining applies to business, headway, and helpful organizations, to make wise urban domains for better associations and better client experience. He investigated about a novel cryptographic way of thinking for checking the enormous information. The creators featured the significance of checking the informational collection away on the cloud and the client's sentiments of fear against the distribution of passed on enlisting. The informational collection away on hazes are ceaselessly arranged to insane access and burglaries. There are two or three top level systems beginning at now set in the state of mind for checking the information on the cloud yet the end client is confirmed from getting a handle on the cloud headway with sureness. With this dread as an inspiration, their work gives a cryptographic system to darken the substance of the informational collection away on the cloud. The work continued with presentation of scattered enlisting condition and its focal concentrations and deterrents close-by the events of certified endeavors utilizing the coursed handling approach for information the authorities purposes. The method works by allocating the files into different groupings and stores the parts unquestionably close-by the isolating check of records which needs part. They named their framework as "Security-Aware Efficient Distributed Storage (SA-EDS)" and the key calculations were called as "Elective Data Distribution" tally, "Secure Efficient Data Distributions (SED2)" figuring and "Convincing Data Conflation (EDCon)" estimation. The structuring looks for after an unmistakable particular proof wherein the standard information and sensitive information were isolated. The typical information is verified utilizing the conventional storing up structure while the delicate information is first broken into two or three fragments and each part is verified self-governingly on a substitute cloud. At the time of recovery, the precarious information from various hazes gets blended and a brief timeframe later moved to the customer who referenced for it. In light of exact assessments, they confirmation to vanquish the security hazards to monstrous information in "coursed enlisting" condition. In any case, it was found in their work that the information is getting isolated into various parts precisely when it is delineated as 'insecure', yet the criteria of affectability was not depicted any place in the recommendation. Moreover, the work implies to store the 'ordinary' information onto a solitary cloud server which is all around that truly matters crazy examining the size of development of information.

Sachidanand and Nirmala(2008) have broke down about the likelihood of Big Data and particular gadgets open in the market to look at unstructured huge information. They have also given isolated data about the examination of Big Data and its criticalness in various fields like helpful organizations, open areas, retail, conveying, and so forth had investigated about central issues like putting away, the chairmen, and preparing attempted to isolate the actualities regarding diabetic dataset and proposed a craving model. Beforehand, Relational Data Base Management Systems was utilized as the information was about nothing, in any case beginning at now, RDBMS can't be utilized as the information is huge.In the current circumstance, by virtue of the immense size of the information and multifaceted nature. The creators battled that tremendous information isn't consistently huge when emerged from little information. They gave a few conditions wherein little information is upheld over giant information to draw much better surmisings. The work began with depicting of each caring conceivable information and some time later the conditions when little information can overwhelm immense information were incorporated. The creators guaranteed that a capable little information is more gainful than a confounded gigantic information standard talking. Similarly, the cost related with administering (acquiring, verifying, checking) huge information is a lot higher when showed up diversely in connection to overseeing little information. Thirdly the heterogeneity and frailty joined with tremendous information makes it multifaceted to oversee. Notwithstanding, no such issues are associated with little information. At long last, the work wrapped up with portraying the issues and inconveniences related with tunneling the pertinent data for the monstrous datasets.

Kiran Kumara Reddi and Indira (2010) have depicted the current colossal information is a get-together of dealt with, semi-made, unstructured homogenous and heterogeneous information. Thusly, they proposed move of enormous extent of information over the system and prescribed new estimations to move Big Data. They worried upon the essential for understanding the key outcomes of tremendous information examination. To lead their examination they included twenty six legitimate examinations. The examination gave a foundation of gigantic information, its structure and examination. The examination got the quantitative framework in which the researchers gathered a few cases from the dealers and resulting to considering and dissecting those case suggested five cases which are set up to handle monstrous information examination inside their structures. The work likewise demonstrated the advantages of getting a handle on colossal information examination in an amazing approach like foundation, operational, upkeep, genuine, administrative and basic parameters under therapeutic space.

Recently Albert Bifet (2005) has mentioned the significance of skilled and snappiest devices to isolate the unfaltering illuminating rundown. At present, gigantic data is made through different sources utilizing web servers to finish up enormous enlightening social affair which structures an impelling assignment to clear significant data out of it in their survey on Big Data portrayed about the Big Data substance, attestation and security of Big Data. The information is developing and finding the opportunity to be sporadic all around requested inciting different inconveniences. The producers examined the frameworks that can be gotten a handle on to conquer the checks in tremendous information structure decisions. They unequivocally rotated around re-attempting the framework, redesignd security, and gigantic information examination limit types of progress. Notwithstanding, they displayed tremendous information and its short history adjacent the qualities of massive information on a fundamental dimension concentrating on volume, course of action and speed. The particular open doors with enormous information were in addition talked about featuring the utilization of tremendous information examination in bearers, Walt Disney, United Parcel Group, and so on. A basic bit of their work was committed to depicting the snags in enormous information advancement assignments. Explicitly explicit foundation, limit, heterogeneity and non-uniform structure of information, security and social hindrances were investigated. At last, condition of-craftsmanship approaches were incorporated into a boundless affiliation which wraps up the work. The cases made by them were not kept up by observational assessments rather just a hypothetical depiction was given by the creators. The plentifulness of giant information gathering framework lies in the manner it deals with the information storing up to such an extent, that the read/ make latencies are at any rate near to a base conceivable reaction time. Since the information tolerates at different areas in a dispersed way, it is fundamental to devise instruments to interface these various objectives with the objective that it looks for after CAP hypothesis (Consistency, Availability and Partition Tolerance). When we talk about coursed orchestrate there exist evident bottlenecks, latencies and surrenders which must be managed reasonably by a normal appropriated information storing up structure. The read/ structure reasonability is a conspicuous factor in the social event of monster information hoarding progression. This induces the frameworks which have better (speedier) read/make points of confinement are favored among others.

Garlasu et.al (2009) have examined the criticalness of cross area figuring which offers the great conditions away limits have broke down about the significance of stage and instruments in the use of helpful organizations industry which can resuscitate their arranging time. He proposed two systems for improving the read/ make execution out of the huge information hoarding structures. Their framework depended upon the spare memory of customer, generally speaking store memory and certain approximations. The work talked about the criticalness of a dispersed structure in passed on enrolling condition near to a concise delineation of pre-getting and holding parts for improving read benefit of the framework. There were two or three suppositions like no correspondence overheads, closeness of withdrew neighborhood and by and large stores, securing is done especially for analyzing and not for making purposes and that the entire record is hung on nearby and generally speaking store memory. They professed to have improved the investigated access time to a specific point which is clear from the observational assessment wrapped up by them. Regardless, there were several openings in their work. Promptly, the suppositions made were absolutely hypothetical as holding the whole document substance on the region store memory is in each down to earth sense unbelievable. For instance, think about a record with a size of 100 GB. In the event that this record is to be investigated, by then the whole 100 GB must be secured which is past the area of innovative personality as the spare memory is very restricted even in the present moment. Therefore their strategy may work fine for negligible size records yet isn't reasonable for immense size reports. In like manner, it was flawed from the substance of the work that the general spare will be available at which focus as no structure diagram was given by them

Sahoo et al.(2016) are of the view that "monster volume of patient information is made each day from power's notes, ace's fix, clinical reports, and body sensors. The examination of human organizations parameters and the longing for the subsequent future flourishing conditions are still in the newborn child engineer. A Cloud empowered Big Data sensible stage is the most ideal approach to manage inquire about the made and unstructured information conveyed from human organizations the board structures." the creators proposed another two-level gathering framework by consolidating the "upper-level in-memory record structure" and "lower-level parallel file framework". They utilized "Tachyon" and "OrangeFS" to manufacture their model. Tychyon is an in-memory report framework made in Java while OrangeFS is an open source record structure which supports parallelism at its center. To delineate their strategy the creators at first incorporated the fundamental working and capacity about information concentrated unparalleled figuring (HPC) flawless models and the related devices and movements utilized in HPC. Their work was away for improving the introduction of HPC when united with Hadoop System. There were two prime classes of focuses in the standard HPC framework. First are "server farms" which store the certifiable information substance and the other are "register focus focuses" which play out the dealing with on these information. In their way of thinking, Tachyon was passed on "process focuses" while OrangeFS was sent on "server farm focuses". OrangeFS has the commitment of tying down a pantomime of the information to recoup if there should rise an occasion of a shortcoming or information mishaps. An illicit relationship of access introductions of the conspicuous HPC working environments was given in their work. The test examination wrapped up by them, broadcasted to improve the throughput of the structure.

Tawalbeh et al.(2016) "the development in PDAs, for example, multi-sensor orchestrated pushed PDAs is likewise utilized as the information gathering contraptions" . "By virtue of colossal extent of patient information gathered, a social assurance Big Data is being created. Hence a quick preparing technique like Cloud figuring circumnavigated point of confinement and managing condition is depended upon to store and process the social insurance information" as portrayed . The creators in evaluated the ceaseless approaches about including noteworthy learning models for gigantic information. The work checked a few use spaces of critical learning headway related to IoT natural structure like social assurance, transportation, utilities for current customer solaces, and so on. The different jobs of huge learning related to enormous information were besides featured in their work. The creators worried upon the point of confinement of noteworthy learning headway to pass on offbeat and ahead of time new information for the enormous datasets which can be fundamental in taking better and educated choice at every estimation. The work besides examined differing critical learning models like CNN, RNN, DBN, and so on. At last, the inconveniences in getting a handle on huge learning frameworks with enormous datasets were incorporated.

Beginning at now, Yu et al.(2016) have detailed that "various information figuring systems have climbed as profitable illustrative gadgets. Many moved procedures and devices have rose in the nonstop past as announced by various producers to dismantle human organizations parameters" has point by point that "for better essential expert by the authorities, the flourishing parameters of get-together of patients are to be looked". The producers in] proposed a cross breed building utilizing a coordination of both electrical and optical structures parts to use scattered handling and Big Data applications. They fought that typical electrical sign affiliations were not appropriate for managing huge datasets and dynamic I/O demands as they eat up huge extent of essentialness. With the progression of IoT improvement, the rate at which the information is made, verified and recovered has broadened exponentially and standard electrical affiliations were unfit to outfit required transmission limits with insignificant latencies and hardships. Another deterrent of electrical affiliations included by them join the tremendous extent of cost attracted with cooling the structure which gets warmed while moving monstrous datasets starting with one affiliation then onto the accompanying in the coursed system. Hence to beat these obstruction their work gave a techniques for optical relationship between the system parts to make the information move quicker while debilitating less extent of vitality. So as to do in that limit, they separated the traffic structure in the server estates running on cloud advancement reliant on essential parameters like group check, information move window measure, section rate, and so on. At long last, they overviewed the introduction by separating their recommendation and the standard and other essentially indistinguishable models. The exploratory outcomes as guaranteed by them can lessen the general expenses of server farms. Unequivocally the work confirmed to improve the yield rate by diminishing it to about 39% while essentially lessening the expense acquired in chilling the structure from 49% to 27%.

Rallapalli et al. (2016) are of the view that "to see the gathering of patients, diseases, and needs, Big Data examination is finished with the help of various AI instruments" are of the propensity that "open systems at present can't do Big Data examination and managing the voluminous standardized savings data. On the other hand, the privilege as of now open front line framework, Cloud stage gives a versatile, parallel and appropriated managing structure and Map Reduce for quick human associations data organizing". The makers in assessed the issues and issues related to heterogeneous titanic data concerning interference domain systems. The maker concentrated on that in order to give a comprehensive viewpoint on the security sections present in the system and the component of their reasonableness, it is crucial to interlink and review security information from heterogeneous sources. This can show to be reasonable for protecting from the diminish security threats that an individual security instrument fails to address. Regardless, the interlinking of these security instruments has a couple of dumbfounding burdens including changed data blueprints, weakness and aggravations in the data, nonattendance of rule frameworks, fear of customer profiling, assurance breaks, etc. Their work gave the outline of the impedance domain structure, its working and modernized security related issues. It further fused the development of AI procedures in the impedance presentation structure and its potential challenges and issues. Finally, the nonattendance of attractive datasets for setting up the structures was found in the work.

Dignitary and Ghemawat (2008) have point by point that "Guide Reduce can process the mammoth volume of data in parallel on Cloud. Fundamental focal motivations behind using Map Reduce framework are the flexibility and change as per inside disappointment during huge data managing. Everything considered, another cross breed model is expected to work in a therapeutic office condition to process and separate the human associations Big Data. In that model, Map Reduce parallel masterminding structure surrounded the standard fragment". The makers in made a review out of various applications and techniques in the field of remote enormous data expressly including data helped transmission, data driven framework redesign, etc. The present time and place of IoT driven progression has seen a smart improvement in course of action of latest development and methods by people in a general sense fluctuating social statuses. Today is advancing pleasantly to express that we are living under the umbrella of IoT improvement as one another thing around us is bit by bit at any rate almost certainly getting related with each other and to us making an enormous IoT regular structure wherein we individuals are in like manner a grungy substance. In order to give a for the most part thorough viewpoint on remote colossal data it was confined into four layers viz. application, structure, transmission and data layers. Also, the procedure of remote data get-together, storing up and examination were discussed. The work was done up by highlighting the security and affirmation issues related to remote gigantic data and the open burdens and research openings were also analyzed.

Lee and Han (2011) have dealt with and proposed "a window based brief data assembling and checking models used to improve the comfort of patient review. In standard healing associations structures, the patient data are gathered, checked and disassembled in a standard manner, which can't invigorate the culmination of complex thriving conditions". In addition, an audit of the evident appropriated system open for overseeing goliath datasets was given along a staggering relationship between's the standard datasets and monstrous datasets. Their work furthermore stressed upon the requirement for seeing huge data and huge data or disturbance ridden circumstances from among the colossal loads of datasets. Considering the heterogeneous and complex nature of these monster datasets, it changes into a shocking endeavor to see which data is colossal and which isn't. Another test that was fused into the work was the beneficial openness of data in the hour of need. Since the datasets are titanic, it is exceedingly confounding and difficult to check for the required data and recoup it from the records. Finally, they in like way highlighted the various wellsprings of therapeutic associations colossal data including electronic structures association, sensors, chronicled records, digitized reports, etc. To address these weights and restraints, the work showed structure to avow social protection data and information of the patients and give a frameworks for influencing and gifted data joint exertion and collection instruments. In order to guarantee the information of the patients, the makers proposed a three-level structure close to a 2-level security framework. The major estimation is in charge of get-together information from various sources in the wake of supporting the customer (patient or expert), the subsequent estimation is for pre-setting up the information got from the past estimation.

Ashwin Belle et al.(2015) have uncovered that "the rapidly making field of Big Data examination has started to recognize a titanic development in the development of therapeutic associations practices and research. It has offered instruments to gather, control, look at, and change monstrous volumes of managed and unstructured data made by current human associations systems. Huge Data examination has been starting late related during the time spent thought improvement and illness examination. Eventually, the appropriation rate and research improvement in this field is so far moderate due to some focal issues inside the Big Data perspective". Starting late they have in like manner discussed a piece of the veritable bothers in the promising spaces of supportive research. In the makers investigated the purposes of constrainment and limit of basic learning structures in achieving improved results in the field of model statement, semantic examination, information recuperations, etc when related with tremendous educational accumulations. The work fused the features, applications and dimension of critical learning in various figuring spaces. The makers in joined the sketchy and relative repercussions of enormous data. In order to reuse the data for future references or making determinations, it must be spared with an authoritative focus on that its consistency remains impeccable every single through it securing lifetime. They further consolidated the issues and burdens for the relationship of relentless data lifecycle close to the need of rule of data so as to perform examination, find openings, see huge and non-fundamental data, absolutely explore. The development of portraying pivotal metadata while utilizing least possible additional room was likewise examined. Issues like data provenance, dependence and between linkages must be especially depicted in order to manage validness, genuineness and consistency. The makers wrapped up with including the need of checking the purpose of imprisonment contraptions and information vaults in order to confirm the data for an intelligently extended time period.

McAfee et al.(2012) have depicted that "Immense Data is a collecting of heterogeneous complex data which requires new gear and programming contraptions to store, free and envision the data adequately. Human associations data is open in various medicinal associations focal motivations behind researchers, helpful organizations consolidation affiliations and government affiliations. In any case, these data are not set up to pass on clearing information to the customers". The makers in consolidated the fundamental for studying the component of monstrous data (for instance how beast is truly called as "colossal") in order to animate its affiliation. Besides, the potential outcomes and ideal conditions of robotized data and information to the degree improving bits of learning for taking essential business decisions were discussed close to the significance of data driven decisions were in like manner seen. Finally, the issues and burdens in the relationship of tremendous data progress from the affiliations perspective were explored. In spite of the way in which that they share some fundamental properties yet the intriguing attributes of huge data is what make it extraordinary or one of a kind. The refinement and uniqueness of tremendous data concerning the standard datasets. They fused the most distant purpose of enormous data to discharge novel points of confinement and characteristics inside the relationship at the best granular estimation. They referenced web-logs, Social media, video streams as the middle flourishing wellspring of gigantic data. Finally, the key partitions between immense data examination and standard data examination were discussed. The development of IoT in improving the end customer settlement is normally observed by the general masses. The contemporary inventive improvements in the field of enrolling are taking an enormous sway and the electronic enablement of standard things and articles is unendingly yet without a doubt changing into a reality. As IoT is getting embedded in standard use articles and things like socks, shirts, watches, coats, vests, tops, shoes, belts, pants, central focuses, etc, the sensors open in these contraptions are fit for performing such different activities which can't be imagined every decade sooner. The sensor introduced in the socks can evaluate the sweat substance and foot temperature to draw in diabetic patients to keep up a vital separation from clearings that can occur in light of foot ulcers. The sensors exhibited in the shirts can get heartbeat rate and can show to be significant for cardiovascular patients. The sensors present in the contact central focuses can check the glucose levels in eyes and trigger the patients and the mending help gathering if there should rise an event of any odd game plans.

Elshazly et al. (2013) have uncovered that "mending imaging offers essential information on life structures of human body and physiology of organs, notwithstanding the status of diseases. The comprehensive number of patients and human associations affiliations has impelled the standard use of PC for steady diagnostics. Decision truly strong systems are moreover made to be sensibly useful in clinical settings. They have analyzed that distinctive concentrations in government disability structures could be improved by using computational frameworks". The makers in analyzed and included the issues, bothers and livelihoods of enormous data produced using the IoT contraptions. The propelling state of-craftsmanship the primary body of these colossal datasets in the surrounded taking care of condition was in like manner inspected. The nature and degree of data passed on by these IoT contraptions is in a general sense gotten to be overseen by old style data overseeing mechanical social events and structures. The various events of IoT data lifecycle like procurement, cleaning, mix, putting away and examination were discussed. Finally, the open issues and squares in enduring and directing IoT degrees of progress were included. The makers in fused the various bits in charge of the wide division of huge data advances and their looking of intrigue. The extension of data and information from faltered sources has opened new portals for the screens for the better understanding and making novel qualities from the data. The different driving parts contiguous the troubles united with the distribution of tremendous data contraptions and strategies were the prime motivation behind get together of their work. Since its start IoT has been an obvious source from where gigantic volumes of data are being passed on and that too at a vivacious rate. The data related to IoT improvement fundamentally records to propelling data that need relentless securing, getting ready and examination. the activity of dispersed figuring for the attainable relationship of tremendous geospatial data was inspected. The issue and bothers of geospatial goliath data the board were joined. The work contemplated four geospatial data models which are climate, land use, getting the hang of mining, and improvement storm.

As shown by Dougherty (2009) "joining remedial pictures data with various types of data can more likely than not diminish the time taken for a confirmation and improve the precision of essential association". "The standard inspiration driving helpful picture examination is to pass on exact and improved interpretation of the disease status to stars and customers" as portrayed. "One of the structures, made for separating and change of monstrous datasets, is Hadoop Map Reduce which gives versatility across over various servers in a Hadoop pack with a collection of occupations". The limits of Myria stack for staggering gigantic data the board. Their work furthermore propels a novel kind of compiler called as "RACO". It was a kind of compiler which is used to streamline the solicitation coming to Myria. The significant focal point of Myria as portrayed by the makers was to direct enormous social datasets. Myria also has the course of action to direct use aloof APIs from inside the system. In their proposed philosophy the standard social variable based math verbalizations were changed over into express API calls. To execute fix up codes, Myria in like way displayed an other solicitation language by the name MyriaL. This solicitation language grants commensurate qualities to the standard PL/SQL language. In any case, MyriaL does not allow data definition language enunciations (DDLS). Everything consolidating the elements in MyriaL is treated as relations. The makers concentrated on that Myria can be in all observes sensibly used as an affiliation to coordinate mammoth datasets as it consolidates each and every required portion inside itself and open to the end customer as an affiliation gathering. Goliath data and scattered figuring are the two most communicated advances in the present time and place diagram. Appropriated dealing with can be used to set up the credits of colossal data to have an extensively far reaching point of view on the tremendous data. The obvious promising shots and businesses of huge data identified with dissipated figuring progress. The work consolidates the giant of goliath data and passed on figuring and the new horizons that can be dealt with using the mix of both the kinds of advancement. The makers discussed the varying wellspring of tremendous data including sensors, IoT, seismic data, splendid data, lead sciences data, etc close-by various troubles related with gigantic data movement (BDT) to the degree acquisition, stockpiling, change, standardization, cementing, security and examination, etc. A boundless examination was given in the work, including the divisions between irrefutably open responses for direct giant data to the degree burdens discussed as of now. Finally, the plans given by coursed planning improvement to the feasible treatment of these tremendous datasets were discussed. The work was done up by highlighting the open research challenges in organizing monstrous data and appropriated figuring

Senior part and Ghemawat (2008) According to "Hadoop Map Reduce is used to build up the speed of tremendous scale strong picture overseeing use-cases". Execution of a snappy system is required in unequivocal applications, for instance, hurt examination in pivotal thought for which Hadoop Map Reduce is the best contraption". In , the makers proposed an instrument of tremendous data storing for heterogeneous gatherings for Hadoop. The proposed EA2 S 2 approach basically, worked by packaging the data and related application occupations as a lone fragment suggested as a pack and instead of giving data and applications self-governingly, they are submitted as a lone part as a party to the structure for overseeing. The fundamental inspiration driving their work was to streamline the data territory. The data was put within spotlights dependent on the randomized computation plan framework made by them. The dynamic data game-plan approach ensures that the pile is decently appropriated over each inside point in the social event. Their perspective works by pre-assessing the wonderful occupations that ought to be done of the concentrations to fittingly put the data things on the data squares of these center core interests. This framework regulated supposition that each server keeps up the metadata about execution times of the occupations consigned to it. This associates in the indisputable confirmation of future assignments subject to honest to goodness execution. The undeniable assessmen

Ohno-Machado et al.(2012) "weight structure is the diminishing of volume of information, keeping up essential parts without losing basic information. In Big information examination this weight system perceive an essential movement in keeping up gigantic volume of information in a compacted structure in information amassing. In spite of the way wherein that different frameworks have been made for strong picture weight, just couple of strategies are basic for Big Data weight". The advancement of epic information in resources the experts was considered in. How beast information examination can be utilized to deal with the positive conditions inside and out more properly abutting the difficulties and issues were talked about. The improvement of AI and information mining structures in resource the authorities was additionally found in the work. The properties of incredible conditions that were confirmed upon join gear accomplishment, steady quality, unexpected structure thwarted expectations, and so forth. The sorting out for resource the experts was besides assessed in their work. A study was done in on the rising gigantic information perfect models. In particular, the improvement of appropriated figuring and its including developments was examined. The work depicted huge information concerning 5 V's and given a clarification of these attributes. Different limitations and lacks of the scattered figuring frameworks for supervising monstrous information were additionally included. At last, some short presentation of shadowiness getting ready and direct picking was given as an improvement to coursed enrolling to vanquish its goals adjoining an inconceivable examination of the three degrees of headway subject to execution parameters like versatility, control structures and system plans and the board. The closeness of epic information has drawn in the affiliations and people to take information driven choices. With colossal information, an ordinarily growing number of experiences are starting at now open dependably utilizing a blend of remarkable examination contraptions which were not utilizing all strategies adequate beginning at now. For instance, an online book shop can screen its client to search for their inclinations and types and send recommendation and suggestion of the books. In like manner, obligation reward can be given to the standard clients and obliged time explanations behind control can be offered to the potential clients. Every single action of the client visiting the online book shop site page can be searched for after and examined to drive promising characteristics from it. All these were absurd with conventional mortar and square based fixed books store.

Yang,et al.(2010) has been made subject to the Hadoop for trading electronic restorative records affirming and sharing among various social security structures. This structure will assist clients with getting restorative pictures from a database as and when required. In this framework, the information is passed on to a Cloud for reason for constrainment, scattering, and preparing. A Cloud organizing model is made and executed. The heterogeneous and spry nature of enormous information makes it hard to manage. The isolated sources, unstructured nature, nonappearance of definition and weakness further add to the multifaceted nature. It is fundamental to comprehend the uncommon properties of monstrous information and think about structures and reacts in due request in regards to fitting relationship of these immense datasets, at totally that point we can outfit the true blue cutoff of massive information to take much better choices which are instant information driven. The producers reviewed the gigantic information chain and gave a square structure to the proportionate wherein stages like information gathering, change, examination and dean were incorporated. At long last, the bits influencing the central ace methodology like nonappearance of coordination, nonattendance of attractive information, mess up, separate in instructive's perspective were broke down. There have been wide hopes to see the potential focal reasons for appropriated figuring based information the board versus conventional joined information the board structures. One such examination was driven utilizing "Unequivocal Sustainability Modeling (OSM)" metric. The different segments that effect the show like indifference, sort out traffic, size of information things, and so forth were seen. The starter evaluation was empowered which included moving and sponsorship up of 10000 reports all of 1GB size while the ensuing examination included moving and support of 1000 record all of 10GB size. In both the cases, coursed figuring development to the degree anyone knows had performed better when ascended out of the standard structure.

Teng et al. (2010) for helpful picture information. The information is traded this model wherein Microsoft Windows Azure is utilized as a Cloud enrolling stage. The presentation of front line sequencing systems in human secured qualities by has made conceivable to apply acquired markers by specialists in a dimension of individuals to see the vast sicknesses. "After the development of normal markers utilizing quality sequencing method, the issue of the hereditary purposes behind the phenotype in turmoil states has been understood through estimations appealingly. Precisely when the human genome groupings and examination was done, it is conceivable to separate characters in charge of different issue over a masses and to give stunning fixes" In] the creators battled that gigantic information and SDN are two most winning advances in right here and now plot. They further investigated that SDN can give legitimately obvious adaptability to the enormous information systems while titanic information can give streamlined and certain game-plan to SDN. By equipping the upsides of titanic information, SDN can be improved to give much better structure choices. The work other than incorporated that SDN can be utilized to improve information transport, dependably direct structure traffic and squares, see support diagrams for information moves, square or drop dirtied information packs, and so forth. Close-by these structure related connection, the creators battle that SDN can in like way be significant in booking of undertakings in beast information the board frameworks.

As distinct **by Treangen and Salzberg, (2012)** and **Koboldt et al.(2013)** . "Titanic Data Analytics of gigantic number of sequencing frameworks in human genomes has made a Big information issue since the human genome contains more than30, 000 characteristics" as sketched out. "A little while later advances are taken to unite clinical information with genomic information which prompts the improvement of Big Data issue" as revealed. These annoys can be managed through computational Big Data examination. The creators analyzed the present referencing frameworks open for tremendous information the board structure. The ideal accessibility and introduction of information is within necessities of constant huge information the board framework correspondingly as the standard mammoth information the executives structures. So as to inspect for the information things from a gigantic heap of information is a heavenly endeavor. Referencing keeps up the metadata about the information so that, it may be recommended and brought utilizing the fast diagram at later stages. The procedures that were destitute down in their work join hashing based perspective, restricted Steiner tree (CST), BTree orchestrated referencing, cross breed B-tree referencing, KR+ - list system, bitmap referencing, padded standard set up together referencing in like way concerning.

Dhavapriya et. Al . (2016) have focused on Map Reduce structure and HDFS in the record referencing with mapping and diminishing in executing Big Data examination. He has proposed a passing on and isolated and the front line distributing framework anticipated Map Reduce to support the database and the maker has depicted the trademark upsides and drawbacks of Map Reduce structure. The makers in concentrated the present referencing systems open for immense data the managers structure. The steady availability and presentation of data is inside necessities of reliable monstrous data the executives structure likewise as the standard immense data the board systems. In order to search for the data things from a colossal load of data is an amazing task. Referencing keeps up the metadata about the data so that, it might be deduced and brought using the record at later stages. The structures that were destitute down in their work wire hashing based framework, unessential steiner tree (CST), BTree formed referencing, crossbreed B-tree referencing, KR+ - record procedure, bitmap referencing, cushioned rule based referencing, etc.

Chen He Ying Lu David Swanson (2010) has developed another framework to invigorate guide undertaking's data locale and interweaved this structure into Hadoop default FIFO scheduler and Hadoop sensible scheduler explained the planning of Map Reduce which works in two phases: map stage and decline orchestrate. They portray how to parallelize and disperse figurings and to make such estimations need tolerant. They have also explained about how execution diminishes the impact of moderate machines and to administer machine foiled desires and data trouble. In , the cloud based inducing gathering frameworks for overseeing remote titanic data were discussed with the help of two cognizant examinations. The solid and versatile nature of dissipated enlisting movement makes it a legitimate validity for coordinating enormous scale spilled datasets as it allows in each judicious sense vast cutoff and figuring limits. This is the reason a lot of the affiliations and attempts are before long benefitting the promising workplaces of passed on enrolling movement. The work inspected the key furthest reaches of streamed figuring near to its affiliations like IaaS, PaaS, SaaS, etc. In addition, a short introduction about private cloud and open cloud was likewise given.

Madhavi Vaidya (2012) has given a chart of Map Reduce programming model, HDFS Architecture, Hadoop Cluster structure and Parallel Map Reduce figurings. The maker has moreover outlined the work arrangement of Map Reduce structure and some enormous issues like change as per non-crucial frustration. With the ascending of 5G improvement, the horizon of colossal data is in addition set to broaden. In any case, the standard systems for 5G area necessities, costs caused meanwhile, limited reach are not legitimate for administering rapidly broadening gigantic data. In setting mindful 5G frameworks was explored by proactively verifying the substance of 5G structures and in setting on this gigantic data arranging was moreover proposed. In their procedure, the makers assembled mammoth datasets to overview the acknowledgment of the substance and simply those substance which cross an edge were held in the BSs. Important learning structures were used to achieve the determinations on omnipresence estimations. The crucial explanation behind this structure was to achieve higher purchaser dedication and backhaul offloading. The work in like manner explored the latest models, bothers and issues of tremendous data managing concerning a noteworthy examination of insignificant data customers in Turkey.

Acharjya and Ahmed (2016) have dismembered about enormous number of instruments that are open to process Big Data and some present methods for investigating Big Data. While looking the Big Data examination with have explained the planning of titanic degree of data for learning disclosure and to get the huge verified information have delineated about the specific data burrowing frameworks for expelling satisfying information from huge data gathering. The makers in proposed a human-driven resource framed structure "Resource Integrated System for Big Data (RISBD)" for persuading most distant purpose of huge data. Their technique uses the available resources of old style work a region structures for checking colossal datasets. They affirmation to lessen the cost recognized in obtaining submitted limit contraptions and spaces with this technique. The work discussed the current goliath data accumulating and the executives parts like Hadoop, RAID, DAS, NAS and SAN to signify things up. The proposed RISBD was a kind of appropriated and related totaling programming methodology subject to XML. Every individual host expected to enroll itself with the server by sharing its securing metadata so the server can likewise spread the datasets among the available social event units to these related and enlisted has. Another piece of room of RISBD that was highlighted in their work joined the cutoff of host structures to go about as a server if the crucial server fails horrendously or terminations out of the blue, in that limit giving reliable limit limits.

Nandakumar and Nandita Yambem (2014) have explained the importance of Apache Hadoop in server homesteads and condemning of moving existing data mining figurings onto Hadoop driving force better parallel getting ready adequacy. An enormous issue with titanic data is the extraction of colossal worth data from among the immense volumes of data. If we can empty quality data, at unequivocally that point we will presumably attainably misuse the upsides of goliath data degrees of progress, by and large, the data is basically a huge garbage dataset. To achieve this target, the makers in proposed a data quality-being utilized model with respect to "ISO/IEC 25000" measures. The proposed model regulated achieving three fundamental properties viz Contextual Adequacy, Temporal Adequacy and Operational Adequacy. The work in like manner progresses the best way to deal with survey the part of data quality. To affirm their system a working model was inspected which relied on the cash related part. In the model, the makers picked see based information as data and see which information among the enormous sets is helpful to focus regards.

Aditya et al. (2012) have point by point about the Big Data issue and its optimal strategy using HDFS for limit and parallel getting ready enormous edifying records using Map Reduce structure. They have done model execution of Hadoop pack; HDFS securing and Map Reduce framework for managing enormous instructive records have seen that Hadoop is the middle stage for managing Big Data. It is relied on to scale up from a single server to a colossal number machines, with a phenomenally abnormal state of progress as per interior disappointment. Unsurprising or in each pragmatic sense diligent examination near to a gifted securing and the board arranging is the need fundamental. A proportional kind of configuration was depicted called by "Starfish". The work consolidated the fundamental for inclination required to tune the introductions of the zone Hadoop structure. With this confinement as a motivation, Starfish was made to give altered tuning of the Hadoop structure with no external hindrance. Starfish depended upon top to Hadoop to give a userfriendly interface and question managing instruments. Starfish performs three game-plans of tuning in the structure unequivocally work technique level, remarkable occupation that ought to be done estimation and business level. It further uses the probability of JIT work streamlining to improve the masterminding of associations.

Huang Lu et al. (2015) delineated about the most focal bits of Hadoop, for instance, HDFS, Map Reduce, and Hbase. Apriori estimation has been done on Apache Hadoop sort out by depicted about the duty of Big Data Analytics and Hadoop to render the relationship of human associations to everyone with flawless cost. With the advancement of science, different applications which rely on iterative checks appear. Hadoop Map Reduce relies on a non-cyclic data stream model. With the yield of the past Map Reduce fill in as the obligation of the going with Map Reduce work, the iterative activities can be entered. In such structure, the data used in each cycle is stress and reprocessed, wasting a lot of time being developed. The makers in proposed "Radoop", a mix of Hadoop and Rapid Miner Tool to give essential executives to managing and detaching huge datasets. The execution nuances and deal frameworks were in like manner given in their work. It in like manner given brief bits of data concerning Hadoop and Map Reduce frameworks. The joining gave in like manner used some inbuilt techniques and fragments of Hive and Mahout. The data in Radoop were confirmed in Hive with the objective that it will all things considered be sensibly tended to upon. The qualification in data into required game plan was performed using HiveQL. The unequivocal evaluation supported that the proposed Radoop approach performs much better than the standard independent Hadoop structure. Glimmer is an open source undertaking made by UC Berkeley AMPLab. With the attestation of a circled memory reflection that empowers draftsmen to perform in-memory depends on colossal social affairs, Spark gives RDD changes and exercises to the customers to use Spark attainably. Sparkle is done in Scala and portrayed as a huge article arranged language with plentiful resources. The rule relationship to offer assistance for Apache whirlwind guarantees Apache Spark as Data Science instrument. Glimmer Reliability can be picked a choice from Intel proposal for blaze to be used in social protection game-plans. Apache Spark is the fast all around strong huge data examination engine and it is absolutely sensible for any kind of enormous data examination. Not long after two conditions, can baffle the fittingness of Apache sparkle are Low Tolerance to Latency basics and deficiency of Memory resources. The gigantic size records are cut into a couple of unclear size humbler lumps. The relentless record squares which hold these humbler variations from the norm are dependably scattered on different circles following the round robin approach. To bind the circles check for overhead, the framework had the approach to enough pick the square size concerning the data. GPFS handles a substitute system for little reports, these records are confirmed in sub-squares which were all around 1/32th the size of the customary square. GPFS grants dynamic and turn back to back data researches. For report questions, GPFS used extensible hashing frameworks. For performing recovery from foreseen dissatisfactions, GPFS gets the instrument of update logs which each center having its own one of a kind remarkable specific log. These logs of different centers are available to one another. This strategy gives an ideal position as any center raise play out the recovery movement if there ought to build up an event of plate disillusionments. In order to avoid stops and manage consistency, each and every conflicting errand were overseen by an other assigned center point which picks the segment of bit of leeway dependent on predefined criteria.

Yan Hu et al (2007) In checking and getting to information from Big Data, Cloud choosing is a pervasive methodology than cook the necessities of remedial associations information and sharing in e-achievement. The examination organizes generally around the execution of SaaS framework to share the social confirmation information. The test results in like manner show the criticalness of SaaS relationship to manage the government disability issues. In any case, clear drawbacks, like detainment of picture sharing and interesting inertness, are up to this point a few troubles for the most part using SaaS relationship to progress development for diabetes the board as portrayed. Programming by the name BOINC was proposed for giving resources and establishment to "open resource preparing endeavors". A point by point depiction of imparted managing to was given in the work. The partitions among P2P and structure selecting were in like manner explained. Similarly, the key focal points of BOINC like purpose of repression free dealing with workplaces, impeccable sharing or resources, pondering composed applications, and repaying were joined. A bit of the occasions of live errands running under BOINC were in like manner given. Adjoining these, the troubles and issues in arranging and recognizing BOINC for the general individuals were discussed and their answers were given here.

Nikhita Reddy and Ugander Reddy (2008) in an examination on Cloud preparing in human associations industry, have uncovered the huge bit of room of using supportive degrees of advancement with Cloud moves. In social protection industry, the specialists can help their patients in evaluating their prosperity condition expecting in every way that really matters zero exertion using Cloud enrolling. In future, utilization of Cloud degrees of advancement in medicinal associations will be especially helpful in the examination and culmination of diabetes mellitus. A creamer approach for achieving higher, versatile and blemish tolerant computational cutoff neighboring perfect access and most remote point frameworks. The system was known as "HadoopDB". The significant explanation behind the proposal was to achieve steady illustrative purposes of imprisonment. The required characteristics for achieving the destinations were seen and included. The recorded establishments of the parallel databases close to their exceptional points of confinement were portrayed here. The proposed HadoopDB works by accessory the individual database structure using Hadoop and play out the MapReduce demand in parallel to achieve higher execution and throughputs. For evaluating the proposed strategy, it was attempted upon the benchmarks like Grep, decision and mix. The results exhibited that HadoopdB positively beats neighborhood Hadoop structure

Yan Hu and Guohua Bai(2009) The study on Cloud selecting e-therapeutic associations by , are of the view that the Cloud progress is used in sharing and overseeing achievement information generally to see troubles and doable Cloud based outlines. The present overview revealed the spellbinding normality of the Cloud regarding Big Data assembling and planning of the inclination that the present model in the restorative field using Cloud preparing theory will bolster patients and experts. The use of Cloud is propelling very much arranged in view of the troubles like security in Cloud-choosing model. A coursed structure named "PNUTS" was depicted. The data in "PNUTS" was checked as hashed tables to give lower latencies, high access rates and surfaces. It gives modified weight changing over the center concentrates close by non concurrent inducing the board. The work puts drives the key essentials and characteristics of an appropriated structure. Close to the assistance for ordinary data types, it in like way supports 'mass' to permit introduction of self-assured structure inside a record. PNUTS was on a fundamental dimension made for serving and overseeing on the web read/make requests overheads and remarkable livelihoods holding up be done. For managing consistency, PNUTS exhibited "per-record course of occasions consistency"

Atiya Parveen et al.(2015) have passed on that E-flourishing Cloud will be the going with immense future in government managed savings parcel. There would be a relationship among the supportive associations providers and customers. In commonplace remedial associations centers, IT establishment will be used most silly with the help of Cloud figuring which would bolster crisis workplaces, aces in like manner as patients to have better treatment. Another circled annal structure called as "Frangipani" was proposed in. It was a two layer building which is exceedingly versatile. The key layer was called as Petal. It was accountable for giving virtual purpose of constrainment frameworks and affiliations. The accompanying layer runs the Frangipani FS on a few center concentrations close to an ordinary Petal gathering. Inside structure of Frangipani is truly fundamental with basic locking of favorable position was done as such as to keep up synchronization and consistency. Another befitting fragment of Frangipani was the changed recovery and the directors with any outside check.

Kyle et al.(2009) are of the end that nowadays human associations industry is likewise amped in the mood for changing the cost, quality, and transport of patient thought things and relationship for any confusion including diabetes using Cloud managing. A Cloud-based structure for individual flourishing record affiliation has been proposed. This structure incorporates self-guaranteeing security framework have portrayed a solution for patient's data aggregate in supportive associations establishments using Cloud figuring. Another framework known as CRUSH was depicted in for in a perfect world hoarding and separating goliath datasets in power obliged conditions. The main inspiration driving CRUSH was to give a certified examination of the power utilization of the favorable circumstances in the passed on social event with the objective that methods can be composed to cleave down centrality impressions. Crush was made in Python which makes it extremely lessened and interoperable application. To help the proposal, an exploratory examination was performed which revealed a few sentiments like: extent of the advancement is conflictingly standing out from significance usage.

Abdullah Al-Malaise Al-Ghamdi et al.(2009) have proposed another Cloud based finding and picking the treatment of diabetes using a Google application engine. This structure is an open source programming, essential for experts and fashioners. This system guarantees security and gives an explanation to cutting edge cell phones and Ipad in an astonishing way have exhibited the e-Health Cloud attainable improvement answer for the therapeutic associations providers. Security challenges in the Cloud arranging is instigating the social event of the Cloud will back off incredibly. As demonstrated by them, future perspective of research will examine the affiliation and utilization of government disability Big Data mining, using Cloud, for improved key expert in human associations.

Vishesh Ved et al. (2010) proposed another electronic data store which gives a street to store pictures like MRI, CAT, X-Ray and diabetic related examination ought to be possible. The comprehensive participation and coordination is required for the emergency standardized savings using Cloud figuring. They have proposed another Cloud based Enterprise Mobility Suite structure called Nefeli Portal. One fundamental regular for the proposed system is the association of Enterprise Mobility Suite structures with other outside structures. The makers in consolidated the controls of Hadoop in genuine relationship of "irrelevant size" records. This joins the records whose sizes are on a very principal measurement not by any stretch of the imagination the default square size of Hadoop. Their technique handles surrounded enlisting perspective for better response time and gave a capable course of action. They depicted the little records subject to relationship among them. This instigates only those record which are connected in a couple or the other way might be set. They independently amassed reports which are "on a fundamental dimension close", "constantly in every way that really matters indistinct" and "absolutely irrelevant records". They used summed up "record joining", "pre-bringing" and "gathering" structures to join the "little reports" together. In a general sense in every way that really matters unclear records are solidified while the magnificently related reports were gathered. Their strategy used three estimation pre-getting away framework. Finally, an examination was done to survey the common sense of document mixing and records gathering procedures.

Shaftab Ahmed and Yasin Akhtar Raja (2013) have depicted about patient checking and e-therapeutic associations activities using long range agreeable correspondence for customers getting a charge out of convenientce and unending accessibility in flourishing and trouble. Deal of e-accommodating associations plans is possible with mobile phones, IPad, and PCs through remote correspondence have explored about the OLA for tremendous dataset on Map Reduce in a Cloud figuring condition. As demonstrated by them, for tremendous scale data planning, OLA could be joined into a Map Reduce and oversaw in Cloud condition. The makers of used the "record measure" as inside parameter to separate different accounts and joined the reports which are underneath past what many would think about conceivable. Further, they used the pre-getting away instrument for improving record get to. Inside qualification found in their philosophy was that no little narrative was allowed to part across over more than two collecting squares paying little respect to whether there were some unfilled spaces left. In the wake of joining the little records, a MapFile was made which stores the approaches of these little reports for their helpful bringing as and when required. The exploring capacity was improved using the pre-bringing segment wherein the metadata was brought truly on the client's store and consequently the referenced data thing can be gotten prompt using this pre-gotten metadata information without the need to urge the Namenode. Finally, the particular examination was done to demand their proposition.

Sreekanth Rallapalli and Augustin Minalkar(2013) have considered that Map Reduce diminishes the cost of getting ready. The social confirmation division has ended up being likewise made in present day world and that the human associations data should be sensibly gutted using Map Reduce. Dissipated taking care of and Big Data in blend can improve the circumstance for the necessities of the present affiliations. Accordingly they have mixed the different advances to get improvement in the zone of social protection affiliations.

Kavitha and S.Kannudurai,(2016) are of the view that "anyway various degrees of progress are used for Big Data organizing with social protection records, available sagacious examination isn't sufficient for all kind of prospering records. Among the open examination, Fuzzy C-prescribes Clustering Algorithm makes driven based assembling from a fixed course of action of models, keeps up all kind of accomplishment data with low costs and gives right intervention to the right patient at the perfect time" . In , the makers put forth a "useful middleware model" named as "Hmfs" for effectively directing "little records". "Hmfs" included three focus parts: "record task interface", "annal the executives" and "report pad" which work in synchronization to consolidate little records. The mixing action was performed by report the affiliation fragment while record pad portion was responsible for streamlining the I/O. The proposed strategy used stand-out piece structure and used pre-getting away strategies to further improve the limit. The makers suggested that Hmfs can be used over HDFS and is helpful for basically saving the Namenode memory overheads as the records were confirmed using in-memory database. The proposed framework other than joined the age of five particular sorts of help for confirming the records at a center position before their joint exertion with HDFS. Hmfs cooks the fundamental functionalities of a data the specialists structure including solidification, deletion, updation and looking of data things or records. They played out the exploratory examination of the proposed methodology and watched it to perform much better when veered from ordinary Hadoop and HAR based techniques.

Recently, **Taylor (2016)** has uncovered that "so far obliged works have been performed on relationship examination of human associations parameters found among different patients. Mortality of emergency division patients in remedial workplaces was anticipated using close-by Big Data-driven AI approach. In instructive perspectives, simply clinical data of patients were considered in the present models disregarding the genuine establishment of weight reactions". The makers in showed an improved difference in HDFS using a "three layer approach" by confining the "UI", "data amassing" and "data orchestrating" layers. The UI layer empowers the customer to move, download or question the report set away in HDFS, the data securing layer is in charge of confirming the veritable data records, and the managing layer is accountable for performing documents capacity dependent on their sizes, joining the documents which are brief time sending the gigantic record indisputably to HDFS gathering. The test assessment showed that the proposed method performed better for record looking at undertaking. Regardless, for the structure improvement, it truly neglect to get needs when demonstrated together particularly in association with customary Hadoop. This was a postponed result of the time go in light of the merging of little records.

Sahoo et al.(2016) have planned a data social event part and relationship examination for the data gathered. Furthermore, they have in like route dealt with a hankering model to predict the future flourishing condition of the patients subject to their present achievement status. The makers in inspected about a document mixing procedure subject to the route frequencies of the records on the cloud. In their system the reports which are gotten to a colossal bit of the time and are little are taken as contender for mixing. They further proposed a data replication approach for beneficially overseeing "little reports" on cloud. They separated the "little annals" into two groupings using "record measure" as an edge regards. Little reports of top tier are those which are under 2MB in size when the square size isn't generally or comparing to 64MB while little records of second groupings are those which are under 10MB in size when the square size is more clear [illegible] MB. In their methodology, the squares are orchestrated i[illegible] [illegible]evel 0, 1 and 2) with varying square sizes at each estim[illegible]. In any case, the squares at same estimation are of same s[illegible] [illegible]uare has some character variable which accomplices in obse[illegible]ing the estimation to which the square has a spot. Squares at level 0 were closest and thus the instructive list away in this estimation had the speediest access. To combine little records they were composed into four sorts on the reason on read/structure works out. The solicitations wire read raised, structure concentrated, read/make genuine, read/make battles.

Weng et al.(2016) have reported that diverse corrupting need models have been proposed in the perpetual past since check of future issue is extraordinarily basic and monstrous for the drugs of patients. Among them, fake neural structure (ANN) systems are astounding and looked into for malady surmise, yet the weight is the getting ready time is longer, and any little change in the data impacts the data managing The makers in proposed an "Improved MapFile based cutoff" procedure which wires "most exceedingly horrifying fit dispersal methodology" for regulating "immaterial size" records. The makers ensure that the proposed procedure lessens the inward brokenness and as prerequisites be builds up the memory utilization of Namenode. The preliminary assessment performed by them exhibited 37% less memory use when veered from old style MapFile approach. The work prepared the establishment of Hadoop nearby the regions and regions of its applications including social alliance destinations, web search devices, etc. It further gave the reasons of substance of little reports in Hadoop and their potential sources close to the issues related with overseeing little records by Hadoop which included consistent I/O, Namenode memory overhead, MapReduce execution contaminations, Network latencies, etc. To consider the working of the proposed approach with other winning structures, the work in like way inspected the systems like HAR, MapFile, and EHDFS, etc. The proposed framework worked by seeing the little size narratives and immense size records from the monster datasets. The gigantic records were indisputably drawn in into HDFS for getting ready while the little reports are first consolidated and some time later gone to the HDFS for managing. The parameters of affiliation taken by the makers wire overseeing time and the proportion of data squares used by Namenode for confirming the little records.

Li, et al. (2015) to plan the EHR data with danger bits to feasibly foresee the osteoporosis and bone breaks have foreseen the heart disappointment by thinking about the physiological data of the patients. Regardless, the verified signs of the torments are not considered in the present need models. As given by "bio-sensors, for instance, ECG, EMG, and EEG are used to store up and transmit the prospering parameters to back-end servers for getting ready. Regardless, the repeat of visits of the patient with the expert and division in a crisis center isn't considered, which has basic impact on the data get-together procedure "have reported that "regardless various pros have proposed the game-plan and recognizing frameworks of the body sensors for get-together data, none of them have developed the data aggregation models of the patients subject to the repeat of visits to an accommodating office" As depicted "a data get-together model has been made using physiological parameters and verified indications of the contaminations of the patients. Furthermore, the association examination is converged with disease need among the patients in a crisis office. Thusly, the fundamental focus of their examination is to demonstrate relationship examination of supportive associations parameters for farsighted examination. They have engineered two relationship examination implies the patients of intra and spread bits of the Hospitals a figuring for imagining future prospering condition of patients subject to their present flourishing status is in like manner dealt with".

Singh et al. (2015) as uncovered by "in medicinal associations structure, some flourishing parameters are enthusiastically associated with each other concerning the contamination and its impact. The connection between the achievement parts are powerfully tangled when a patient has a spot with at any rate two divisions in an inside for examination. An interrelation-dispatch between the patients having differentiating thriving parameters and disease is found. As such, two sorts of examination have performed for relationship assessment, using MapReduce, i.e., intra-pack and between get-together examination". Concurring to,"in intra-pack relationship, the patients inside a for all intents and purposes indistinguishable office are amassed subject to their likeness. In the midst of pack association the likeness or uniqueness of patients in different workplaces" is penniless down.

Mukaka (2012) in that, the future prospering status of the patients, in setting on their present achievement parameters, is anticipated. The patients are amassed in an illuminating party in a particular office reliant on their related traits. Starting late, have articulated that "a FHCP estimation is organized by to anticipate the future achievement condition of the patients subject to their present flourishing status with the precision of 98%.Also, Cloud-based Map Reduce model is used as the overseeing framework for Big Data examination. It is seen that this show can be used for various applications related to accommodating associations and patient viewing, for instance, coronary pain need or hazard genuineness gathering".

Prajesh P Anchalia et al (2015) It is an unsupervised structure used to bundle semi shaped and unstructured lighting up reports. This is one of the broadly used no doubt appreciated and practical figuring's to sort out data have outlined the K-deduces execution on Hadoop arranges. The course to the execution of the figuring and the strategies pulled in with the utilization has been delineated.

Aditya B. Patelet al (2012), reports the major handle the Big data issues. It outline the perfect approaches using Hadoop gathering, Hadoop Distributed File System (HDFS) for most extreme and Map Reduce programming structure for parallel managing to process massive edifying records.

Mukherjee, A. et al (2012) granted that Big data examination group the examination of massive degree of data to get the solid information and reveal the verified models. Gigantic data examination recommends the Map-Reduce Framework which is made by the Google. Apache Hadoop is the open source orchestrate which is used with the certified objective of affirmation of Google's Map-Reduce Model. In this the presentation of SF-CFS is isolated and the HDFS using the SWIM by the face book occupation looks for after .SWIM contains the astonishing heaps of thousands of livelihoods with complex data landing and figuring structures.

Garlasu D et al (2013) Producers fulfilled that Grid Computing offered the favored position about the most far off point limits and the sorting out power and the Hadoop progress is utilized for the use reason. Framework Computing gives dispersed figuring. The upside of Grid figuring focus is the high verifying most extreme and the high supervising force. Structure Computing makes the immense duties among the watchful research, help the masters to separate and store the titanic and complex information.

Sagiroglu Set et al (2013) depict the monstrous information content, its enlargement, frameworks, tests, flawless conditions and irritates of Data. The essential issue about the Big information is the request and security. Epic information tests clarify the survey about nature, conventional science and research Life sciences, and so on. By this paper, we can wrap up that any relationship in any industry having colossal information can get the bit of breathing room from its careful examination for the key thinking reason. Utilizing Knowledge Discovery from the Big information simple to get the data from the confounding enlightening records. The general Evaluation portray that the information is making and persuading the chance to be multifaceted. The test isn't just to aggregate and run the information in like manner how to uncover the obliging data from that amassed information. As exhibited by the Intel IT Center, there are different moves identified with Big Data which are information development, information foundation, information run, information understanding, information speed.

Ling Liu et al (2013) clarified that the information stars, we live in captivating occasions. Information has been the No. 1 quickly making scene on the Internet for the most recent decade. Enormous information examination have the typical to uncover significant bits of learning checked by colossal information that beats the standard most inaccessible scopes of existing frameworks, for example, look sway among clients, revealed by inquiring about customers' dealings, social and land information. In the previous 40 years, information was on a very basic level used to search for after and record business exercises and reliable occasions, and in the going with 40 years information will be utilized despite get new experiences, to control business choices and to flood clear introduction. The key test is to give the correct stages and contraptions to profit by epic information clear and fundamental. In this key note talk, I will find reuse openings and weights from various estimations towards passing on epic information examination as a connection.

Keith C.C. Chan (2013) clarified that the Big Data proposes edifying records that are so mammoth and lift that common information overseeing gadgets and improvements can't change according to. The course toward testing such information to reveal covered models in them is suggested as Big Data Analytics. Medication colleague is associated with monstrous information examination as the structure may require the outline, undertaking and examination of radiantly epic volume of made and unstructured biomedical information beginning from a wide dimension of examinations and studies amassed by emergency focuses, investigate working conditions, pharmaceutical affiliations or even electronic frameworks affiliation. These information may wire sequencing and quality verbalization information, quiet information including sub-atomic information, protein and medication joint exertion information, clinical preliminary and electronic patient record information, quiet lead and self-revealing information in online life, administrative watching information, and dynamic works where models and solution repurposing and protein-protein interface information might be found.

Roger Schell (2013) clarified that the Big information discovers performing count and database endeavors for tremendous degrees of information, remotely from the information proprietor's endeavor. Since a key thought of brute information is access to information from different and affected spaces, security and confirmation will perceive a key improvement in gigantic information creative work. Utilizing titanic information requires access from any zone to information in that space, or some other space it is guaranteed to get to. In the security heading report CSA delineate three undeniable sorts of cloud dependent on the affiliations they give, that are IaaS, PaaS and SaaS. IaaS gives PC foundation that join processor for setting up any application, extra space for disquieting information and structures relationship to clients, for example, Amazon EC2. PaaS gives figuring stage that guide progression, testing and plan of an application with the equipment and programming that is open to the maker at stunningly irrelevant effort and basically decreased of getting and dealing with the gadget and programming, for instance Google App Engine. This circuits support for the vast majority of the structures that are required for improvement, testing and strategy of associations that work over the Internet. SaaS, is a cloud model where everything required for the working of the application that solidification the thing and its related information are checked in the remote structure with the bit of cloud and got to utilizing Internet by clients by methods for undertakings. This examination began with the head of encompassed setting up that might be considered as a novel kind of passed on structure

Shunmei Meng; WanchunDou; Xuyun Zhang; Jinjun Chen; (Dec. 2013)" Big Data Applications" clarified that Service recommender frameworks have been radiated an impression of being gigantic instruments for giving fitting proposition to clients. In the most recent decade, the level of clients, affiliations and online data has developed quickly, yielding the beast information examination issue for connection recommender structures. As such, standard connection recommender frameworks a tremendous bit of the time experience the slippery effects of adaptability and wastefulness issues when sorting out or dismantling such epic scale information. Moreover, a large portion of introduced association recommender frameworks present close examinations and rankings of relationship to various clients without thinking about different clients' tendencies, and in like way neglects to get clients' fixed together necessities.

Xingdong Wu; Xingquan Zhu; Gong-Qing Wu; Wei (VOL.26, January 2014), "Information Mining with Big Data" clarified that Big Data concern beast volume, shocking, making illuminating files with various, free sources. With the down to earth headway of structures connection, information verifying, and the information social occasion limit, Big Data are after a short time quickly making in all science and building spaces, including physical, ordinary and biomedical sciences. This paper demonstrates a HACE theory that delineates the highlights of the Big Data revolt, and proposes a Big Data arranging model, from the information mining point of view. This information driven model cements referencing driven blend of data sources, mining and study, client centrality appearing, and security thoughts. We consider the enraging issues in the information driven model other than in the Big Data change. While the term Big Data truly worries over information volumes, our HACE theory underpins that the key properties of the Big Data are 1) epic with heterogeneous and various information sources, 2) free with dispersed and decentralized control, and 3) unfathomable and making in information and learning affiliations. Such joined qualities suggest that Big Data need a ¯big mind to join information for most fundamental properties.

Shan Suthaharan clarified that the particular issue of Big Data depiction of structure bother traffic. It talks about the structure weights offered by the Big Data issues related with system obstruction measure. The craving for a conceivable impedance get in a system requires immovable accumulating of traffic information and learning of their properties on the fly. The procedure on gathering of traffic information by the structure prompts Big Data issues that are rehearsed by the volume, amassed combination and speed properties of Big Data. The learning of the system characteristics requires AI procedures that catch guideline speaking information of the traffic structures. The Big Data properties will impel pivotal framework weights to perceive AI structures.

Ahmed E. Yourself et al (2014) explained that in this paper we begin a structure for Healthcare Information Systems (HISs) in setting on enormous data examination in versatile appropriated enlisting conditions. This framework gives an anomalous condition of mixing, interoperability, responsiveness and sharing of accommodating associations data among human associations providers, patients, and experts. Electronic Medical Records (EMRs) of patients scattered among different Care Delivery Organizations (CDOs) are joined and set away in the Cloud accumulating a region; this makes an Electronic Health Records

(EHRs) for each patient. Adaptable Cloud allows exuberant Internet access and space of EHRs from wherever and at whatever point by systems for different stages.

Ashwin Belleet et al (2015) explained that the rapidly extending field of colossal data examination has endless to recognize a true work in the development of accommodating associations practices and research. It has offered contraptions to assemble, direct, examine and join enormous volumes of various, made, and unstructured data made by current healing associations structures. Colossal data examination has been starting late related towards helping the technique of thought transport and disease examination. Dissipated planning is the spot one server or a great deal of servers make the enlisting at one spot for various servers that are found somewhere else that are associated using the Internet. As showed up by Reese , cloud is the spot one can use any progress remotely, with no foundation at its machine, and it may never pay for this if it don't use this improvement. The cloud can be regular as a basic scattered structure , which host different affiliations and give these relationship to each and every customer over the world using Internet. These affiliations are used for enabling different applications at various server living arrangements including reasonable gear and structure programming.

Ho Ting Wong et al (2015) explained that the immense data is a strongly discussed issue in the sharp zone, and government disability pros are obviously not a confinement. This article intends to give a show in emergency course of action research to reveal the upsides of driving such research using enormous data. Immense data is a novel and supportive research approach, and emergency prescription experts could maltreatment by using this system and by doing everything thought about makes great research at a speedier pace. Gigantic data, of course, gives adaptability in inspecting an instructive party from exchange perspectives. In like manner, in light of the manner in which that administrative relationship starting at now keep up a great deal of immense data, look at using gigantic data can be created effectively.

Tanenbaum, A. S. (2007) Distributed Systems: Principles and Paradigms grants that a coursed structure is a sum of autonomous PCs everything considered heterogeneous that appears to its customers as a lone structure. Cleared with the stray pieces of passed on figuring, in which different free dealing with contraption work so they transmit an impression of being a singular PC that improve the utilization of existing resources with express undertakings as it's been said.

Warren Smith and Chaumin Hu (2004) spread the examination report by the name An Execution Service for Grid Computing covers the detail for improvement from scattered to network choosing. As showed up by this report, consequent stage to the appropriated preparing was system choosing, where the experts handle particular thought using which the spilled structure can be given to the customer as a single structure. In this the idea was to work upon the central focuses that are open in the underutilized structure, and can be given to the outside (remote) customer. It interlaces the work on different examinations subject to the occupations of getting ready power, employments of memory (key and associate) and avowing them.Ian Foster et al. appropriated the paper Cloud Computing and Grid Computing 360-Degree Compared and age by seyyad mohsen and amidst (2012) named Cloud managing Vs. Cross area Computing clears the pivotal of coursed getting ready in setting to ordinary choosing. This papers other than clear how spread planning is astounding in relationship with system selecting, that give the cleared thought of streamed enrolling.

Lijun Mei et al. (2008) in their examination appropriated in A Tale of Clouds: Paradigm Comparisons and Some Thoughts on Research Issues gave a dynamic relationship of different expecting that circuit streamed figuring, unavoidable preparing and affiliation selecting. They shut their examination with the structure spots of the hovered selecting on the central model of PC building, including three explicit features: input-yield, hoarding and tally. The maker showed an examination for most of the three features that can be thick as: (I) the information yield feature of PC building takes after with that of affiliation dealing with in appropriated selecting. (ii) The purpose of repression feature of PC arrangement is close to that of certain figuring than that of affiliation choosing scattered dealing with. (iii) The estimation features of these perfect models are same. As needs be, in setting on their relationship, makers give differing exploration issues that wire particular pluggable figuring central focuses for cloud applications, straightforwardness in access of data, versatile nature of employments in cloud condition, and revamp estimation of usage quality in cloud.

Sangwan and Singh (2016) in their creation Services and Security Aspects in Cloud Computing analyzed appropriated figuring and sorts of fogs. Non-reasonable, cash related and creative perspectives to be tended to by fogs are relatively given in the paper. The examination of dissipated enrolling affiliation models-Software as a Service (SaaS), Platform as a Service (PaaS) and Infrastructure as a Service (IaaS) is done in the paper. Finally this paper gives particular security issues are given in the game plan. On the off chance that there ought to build up an event of open cloud both the issues are in like way fundamental as in setting of data security, the data is confirmed in a structure which is available to the general individuals that is anybody can get to any data if not check suitably, what's more the data use Internet, so anybody that is on the framework can get to the data and use this data. While if there should rise an event of private cloud, data isn't available to open. Fundamentally the customer from a specific social affair are sponsorship to get to the data in the cloud, so data is secure to some degree while for using this data, part use open structure called Internet so the framework security is as yet an issue. In case moving to cross breed cloud, IT controllers picks the best mix of open cloud and private cloud affiliations, similarly as the right cloud ace association, that meet their specific and business goals.

Sean Carlin et al. (2012) in their dispersing-Cloud Computing Technologies give the nuances of some key characteristics of the appropriated selecting developments, and explain the three fundamental affiliations named Software as an affiliation, Platform as an affiliation, Infrastructure as a relationship of the coursed figuring structure that portrays the spread dealing with headway and their vehicle model. In this maker have seen and explained the genuine improvement of virtualization that makes passed on getting ready possible. It examined and discussed different troubles that passed on enrolling developments is standing up to now well ordered. In setting on their examination they give the future direction of spread taking care of kinds of advancement close by various applications that may use the cloud and models, it search for after. It gives a short perspective of the course wherein the progression will proceed into the future and how.

C. Weinhardt et al. (2009) in the spread-Cloud Computing – A Classification, Business Models and Research Directions talk about the advancement of hovered figuring from structure preparing. In light of their examination, makers discusses upon the technique structure. In this paper makers talk about the specific model used for sending of cloud. It gives different affiliations that are using different models for their distinctive business applications. In the wake of getting the nuances of properties, affiliation model and association model the going with occupation was to get the learning of the working of different fogs with the objective that its sensible use can be made. The report from NIST (2011) by the name ¯NIST Cloud Computing Standards Roadmap is huge in understanding the working of cloud. As showed up by OSI model cryptography is used at the application layer if there ought to be an event of data transmission. The customer can pick any way of thinking for data security that is open today depending upon its need. In the data transmission structure security is the bit of the physical layer. Most of the layers over the physical layers foresee that an OK business ought to accomplish the security of data on the framework. Affirmation is performed on some layer agreeing to the framework picked by coordinator. For the security of structure, the advancement be done at the physical layer join dissatisfaction revelation, strike an area and vigilant countermeasure systems.

Ang Li *et al.* (2010) in the age -Cloud Cmp: Comparing Public Cloud Providers work with various open cloud providers, in setting on their examinations make Cloud Cmp, which is a structure that work on the powerful relationship in execution and cost of cloud providers. In setting on the estimations that relies on the impact on the introduction of customer applications, CloudCmp measures the various parameters offered from a cloud including adaptable figuring, energized purpose of imprisonment, and structures affiliation affiliations. CloudCmp endeavors to ensure sensibility, representativeness, and consistence of these measures while work under the inspirations driving constrainment of estimation cost. Applying CloudCmp to various without a doubt understood cloud providers that together record for winning piece of the cloud customers today, expert thought about that their offered affiliations falter subject to the introduction and costs, so it give them a phase that help in assertion of the best of provider according to the essential. From these executive cloud applications as the critical examinations, they exhibit that CloudCmp can arrange customers in picking the best performing provider for their specific application.

Salman A. Baset (2012) in the paper-Cloud SLAs: Present and Future considers unmistakable open cloud ace connection that consolidation the most recognizable cloud provider named Amazon, Rackspace, Microsoft windows purplish blue and Storm on Demand, check their SLA and wrap up the impact of SLA on the affiliations given by these expert alliance. For this it join particular parameter. It wrap up with the results that from cloud providers which they assessed, no one offer any presentation guarantees for figuring of affiliations and requesting customer to see encroachment from SLA that finds it is the devotion of the customer to raise the issue of SLA encroachment and show it from the affiliations used.Next part in the process was to get some detail of cross breed cloud model that is the mix of two evident sorts of fogs fundamentally one open and another private cloud. We get a few nuances for open cloud from while the information about the private cloud we get the information from making given by different affiliations like HP, Intel and Microsoft. Regardless, one thing was apparent that a huge amount of ace alliance are there for giving the relationship of private cloud yet everything considered most by far of them use some open source cloud programming that are OpenNebula, OpenStack, CloudStack , 2.xetc.Once aware of open and private cloud next business was to interface them for which some record from vmware.com used on the thing vCloud. Some open source cloud programming in like manner gives the module to interface with the open cloud. The latest in this arrangement is OpenNebula that pronounced its thing module for the fragile layer that is cloud programming from IBM \.Next in the process is to get capacity with some security issues in open cloud and private cloud and later check them in the mutt cloud. Before the perspective on security issue in coursed figuring, we need to esteem the security issue in made structure. As showed up by the examination on framework security while working up the ensured structure, following are the concentrations to be considered: Access, Confidentiality, Authentication, Integrity and Non-revoking

Arshad Hashmi et al. (2016) in their dispersing titled-A Survey on Security Patterns and Issues in Cloud Computing Environment give the affirmation that passed on figuring has different focal concentrations yet the security concerns hamper the customer to understand it unendingly. It is undeniable realities for all customers concerning the security risks winning in the cloud. Various customers can no uncertainty offer same physical resources by strategies for multi-residency and virtualization. In any case, this prompts cloud unequivocal perils. Different ensured issues make related to customers data and application by morals of the land measurement of passed on figuring. Owner coalition has the bound definitive control because of this supervising character and finding the opportunity to control have a spot with a modernized resource of the association have seeing shapes in dissipated enlisting. The security dangers which go under sharing, virtualization, and open cloud have been clarified and ensuing systems have been showed up as a counter measure. The security affiliation degree has been unequivocally highlighted in the present examination passed on by improved methodology.

Mahmood (2011) in the examination paper Data Location and Security Issues in Cloud Computing highlights different issues related to data security in the cloud. Maker looks at some condition set up together issues that are based concerning the district of data and its transmission beginning with a one zone then onto the going with. The issues related to zone are crucial in context on past what many would think about conceivable, on account of which end customer needs that data should live in its country. In context on the approachs, standards and foundations of different countries pulled in with data creation, usage and most extreme, movement of data beginning with one country then onto the following may affect these certifiable threats. Another problematic issue is related to availability of data the detachment of data prompts division of the affiliation or application control power outages, inevitable result of this can be loss of customer, and thusly pay and consistency. This examination paper talk around one progressively basic security issue is that is data security in convenientce, which means when the data adaptability is high, the risks related to its security are more, unequivocally, when the data is transmitted begin with one country then onto the going with country and both the countries are regulated by different complete framework.

S. Subashini et al. (2010) in the examination dispersing -A Survey on Security Issues in Service Delivery Models of Cloud Computing [38] explain its finding as dissipated figuring is a way using which the reason for control of managing can be expanded exponentially or the breaking points can be intertwined effectively that is too with no vitality for structure, or getting ready of existing work power, or obtaining licenses of any present programming. So the end is spread figuring can broaden Information Technology's (IT) existing cutoff points with least of undertakings. To complete the piece review for this examination, learning of open cloud, private cloud, cross breed cloud and a bit of the security issue are gathered from above examinations. The security issues in cloud join limit security, middleware security, plan security and application security that is a delayed consequence of the proximity cycle of data in cloud. On the off chance that there ought to build up an event of mutt cloud we attempt to deal with the issue of security at the segment of data by taking some open cloud and executing some private cloud and passing on some application at the segment of their joining - cross breed cloud.

He coursed a paper titled Network security: it's an unprecedented chance to focus on it. As showed up by their vehicle data security is the perspective that empowers a client's colossal data to be changed to grungy data that can be transmitted. In case this foul data is hacked and gotten by the item engineer during transmission, a key is requiring to decoding the real and satisfying data. The course toward using key for security is noteworthy to certain estimation since strong cryptographic key of the past are incredibly easy to break now well ordered by the use of astoundingly brilliant PC, so the key of present will leave date in not very far-evacuated future.

L. Wei et al. (2013) in the paper-Security and Privacy for Storage and Computation in Cloud Computing [39], proposed a show used for studying of data security in the cloud and given the name Sec Cloud, that weakens insurance conning and secure the figuring. As shown by the maker it is the latest procedure that together considers both the issues, first issue being the issue of security in data securing and another is estimation examining of security in the cloud. Investigators have given the structures to both these security issues and propose the show named SecCloud that they use to achieve the individual goal. They prescribe that to improve the productivity of the show, different customers' referencing must be meanwhile overseen through the social affair check. By the broad security examination and execution preoccupation in Sec HDFS, another show proposed by the maker results are conceivable and able for achieving an ensured dissipated figuring. In the last one and a half decade, spread enlisting has produced using being a promising business thought being used by the relationship inside for its very own unique usage to one of the speediest making space of the IT business where this focal points can be given as the relationship to outside world on pay per use premise. Notwithstanding various hypes joining the cloud, experience customers are spellbound to pass on their business in the cloud in context on the central focuses it suits the undertaking. Security is the basic issues which is carrying on as a bottleneck in the movement of dispersed enlisting. Another issue is related to issues with data security and data affirmation that continue plagueing the market. The structure of cloud other than has a fundamental hazard to the security of the cloud condition on account of the risk in existing headways. In this paper maker proposes to the customers that they ought to be watchful in getting.

Hanqian Wu *et al.* (2010) in the distribution -Network Security for Virtual Machine in Cloud Computing [40] discusses on framework security for virtual machines and for the examination masters select the open source undertaking, Xen, and use this hypervisor as the phase for the predefined investigate. According to this age makers separate the structure security issues that exists in virtual machines, present a novel virtual framework model which cancontrol the intercommunication among various virtual machine events running on the hypervisor with better security. From the bit of security, one essential test in the engineering of an appropriated planning stage is that of interconnectivity between various virtual machine events. As if customers who are surrendered super customer access to their provisioned virtual machine, without genuine thought or coincidentally, may maybe screen any of the virtual machine or access the secured framework interfaces.

Zhifeng Xiao et al. (2013) in "Statement and Privacy in Cloud Computing" , looks cloud building, its characteristics and the security issues. The different security properties it discusses circuit perplex, legitimacy. The makers make the discussion on cloud plan and enduring quality concerning the threats and framework used for its assurance. The makers inspect various frameworks used for data trustworthiness that joins PDP, POR, Scalable PDP, Dynamis PDP and HAIL . In this age maker looks at cloud commitment and cloud security. It gives an unprecedented view on various strategies of assurance support that breakers information driven security, thought enlisting and cryptographic shows in their examination appropriated in Security Protocols over Open Networks and Distributed Systems: Formal Methods for their Analysis, Design, and Verification gave a framework of usage of formal approachs for the examination and request of cryptographic shows in present day time. Investigators delineate the techniques that are profitable at different fragments of reflection. In setting on their examinations, choice can be drawn that the examination structure is pushing toward making gadgets that expel easy to make subtleties from shows reliant on the ordinary properties and quickly perform formal examinations checking for disappointments of these shows, with the objective that they can achieve their optimal properties. From the point of view of security show facilitator, the examination plan, advancing toward developing dynamically reasonable methods to structure exhibits that will without a doubt be strong and authentically regardless, has executed the mix approach.

Mazhar Ali et al. (2015) in the examination spread-Security in Cloud Computing: Opportunities and Challenges outlines the conceivable aftereffect of their examination that is an outcome of the security issues subject to the ordinary, virtualized, and open nature of the dispersed dealing with perspective. Thusly, the association of this paper gives the counter measures to the issue of security. In this spread examination of the exhibited systems joins the dimension of security affiliations given by the methodologies it investigated. As displayed by the maker their totaled work will immensely help the future prodigies with looking separate the focal concentrations and heaps of their examination tries. The examination of the showed methodology has given the ways to deal with oversee highlight some open issues that drive the examination compose and the astute framework to think as for this issue.

Schiffman, J. et al. (2013) in the age "Cloud Verifier: Verifiable Auditing Provider for IaaS Clouds", give the Cloud Verifier, a structure that cloud shipper can game plan to give cloud checking relationship in IaaS fogs. The cloud verifier is a self-managing relationship in the cloud that can be used to fix a cloud manager's uprightness criteria over the cloud separates. In this examination makers pursues a proof of cloud verifier for the open source cloud stage named Open Stack and demonstrated a couple checking decisions that customers can use to keep up the strong state of their models. The makers work with this structure on two of the most excellent application events used in Amazon's EC2 cloud. As displayed by the examination did by makers the results show unimportant overhead by the cases in context on review finished on more than 20,000 synchronous customers.

Pitropakis, N. et al. (2013) in "It might be All inside the Cloud: Reviewing Cloud achievement" [50], portray how appropriated taking care of is dislodging standard IT establishments all around referenced. By some coincidence, one of the inconveniences that have move by systems for that turmoil is the upkeep of the structure and lacking section of security for the establishment. According to the makers, different operators are working inside the requesting of cloud security and affirmation guarantee, proposing different plans that handle the threats towards cloud structures.

Alabool et al. (2014) in "Traditional trust Standards for IaaS Cloud Analysis and Resolution", portray, as IaaS cloud alliance model breezes up being effectively controlling to all partners, the assessment on the level of trust of the IaaS cloud remains a weight. This advancement learning of targets to watch and pick the crucial perceive benchmarks (CTC) from setting headquartered perceive and setting composed cloud and later masterminded, examined, when put straightaway, and assembled a related mannequin of CTC in a sensible way. The most fundamental inspirations driving CTC mannequin are to give Cloud Service Requesters (CSRs) with a CTC with which to evaluate the part of perceive that can be arranged in IaaS cloud to equip steerage to Cloud Service Providers (CSPs) about what to combine with their new, all around open depended on IaaS cloud, to have the decision to satisfy trust central focuses. To make a move, a sharp examination on setting set up perceives and setting headquartered cloud is given. The results showed that there was a central technique of perceive models in each handy sense vague from Integrity and reputation that were uncared for from the present research related to cloud.

Hazarika et al. (2014) in "The Mobile-Cloud Computing (MCC) Roadblocks", depict cloud managing as a best theory suspected and before now a long time this course has detonated genuinely into a fundamental zone in IT collusion. Experiences, paying little regard to estimation, have each gotten cloud or wanting to attempt cloud. In most recent Smartphone dissect, cell science is a high measure run well with to effect cloud work, the later consistently managing the purposes behind confinement of the past. With cloud work, obliges and related refinement can even be offloaded to cloud and the prepared understanding will in like way be utilized by systems for cell contraptions. This sort of stimulated effort is reasonably called as cell cloud work. To make the steady cloud customary structure to work impeccably is a monster attempt with no other individual. Suffering cloud deciphers putting industry chief motivations behind confinement and touchy information out to a far off cloud merchant, which has most basic security recommendation. With telephone devices, the hazard can be more certified than at whatever point in constant memory. This sort of paper takes a gander at the sensibly a huge number cell cloud troubles that reason cutoff focuses brief courses for PDA cloud upheld effort.

Madhusudan KL ***et al.*** **(2013)** in the dispersing-Data Security Issues in Cloud Contact Center as a Service – A Review derives that cloud security joins by far most of the more orchestrated and got a handle on issues including framework and all other infrastructural vulnerabilities, underwriting, customer access, and affirmation. It similarly joins concerns got from new developments that are found the opportunity to offer the palatable resources (fundamentally virtualized ones), affiliations and accomplice contraptions used to make cloud. These issues are bifurcated by vulnerabilities in hypervisors, physical district of data and veritable viewpoints related with it, and loss of the relationship of data, security and even key action. As cloud needs standard, so in the wake of moving data from neighborhood theory to the structures into the cloud, the nonappearance of standards for shows and plans indisputably influence an undertaking to move to a substitute provider. Progression beginning with one cloud then onto the going with cloud is dangerous, paying little respect to whether advancement is instigated by affirmed reasons that breaker non fulfillment of affiliation level understandings and power outages by ace core interest. All things considered, the standard choice must be deliberately made, as SLAs are not faultless and affiliations control power outages happen at a close speed that is the pace of bit of leeway sharing, multi residency and flexibility that are not dissatisfaction affirmation. After that is made, future improvements of relationship among cloud can be incredibly dazzling like time and costs. As shown by the maker, the endeavor of headway will require a wide work that joins passing on most of the data and resources for a close-by establishment from the present cloud before redeploying to another cloud. In this improvement, various issues still need amazing examination effort, especially those related to affirm virtualization.

Selvakumar, C. et al. (2013) in "PDDS - Making Improvements to Cloud Information Storage Protection using Knowledge Partitioning Method", the makers blueprint passed on aggregating structure licenses checking of learning inside the cloud server successfully and makes the customer to work with the information with none condition of the focal points. Inside the present procedure, the data are confirmed in the cloud using dynamic learning task with computation which makes the client must make a copy for further reviving and verification of the data hardship. An effective dispersed most extreme seeing segment is insightful which over comes the cutoff centers in dealing with the information disaster. In this paper the allocating is proposed for the data gathering which keeps up a key division from the fundamental emulate at the customer side by technique for using scattering structure. This framework ensures outlandish appropriated gathering uprightness, dynamically evident mishandle control and steady unquestionable confirmation of acting astutely server. To achieve this, faraway information dependability checking recommendation is used to produce the feature of passed on putting away. In nature the information are dynamic in cloud. In like manner this work would like to give retailer the information in lessened space with less time and computational cost.

Deyan Chen and Hong Zhao (2012) in their examinations spread in the examination paper Data Security and Privacy Protection Issues in Cloud Computing contemplated that due to the Availability of various model subject to affiliations and sending, and boss features of the dissipated taking care of, data security and security confirmation issues are the bona fide nerves that ought to be settled at the most solid shot. As showed up by the impression of the maker, the issue of security and insurance exist at all the estimations in SPI transport models and in most of the seasons of data life cycle in cloud. The genuine test in sharing data is security insistence that joins guaranteeing lone information. Essential structures that require security certification are generally web business and thriving related systems, in light of their need that union securing of work control information including Visas information and social protection structures with most of the data related to progress. The ability to control the improvement of information and reveal the development of the customer, who can get to that information over the Internet, has changed into a basic concern. These weights entwine which of the individual information can be checked or explored by untouchables with no consent, or whether pariahs can look for after the zones someone has visited. Another weight is whether objectives which are visited by the customer gather, store, and conceivably share specific information about its customers. The most ideal approach to manage security affirmation in the cloud condition is the authentic system for segment of fragile work control data from non-dubious data searched for after by the encryption of tricky segments over the different events of the data lifecycle.

Yongzhi Wang et al. (2013) in the examination creation "Unfaltering quality MR: Integrity Assurance Framework for Huge Knowledge Analytics and Management Purposes" [56] thought about that gigantic information examination and potential relationship of this data is changing into a charming subject with the latest developments used for scattered enrolling and epic information figuring model contrasting with MapReduce. Regardless, tremendous scale get-together of MapReduce applications on open hazes is maintained a strategic distance from by philosophy for the nonattendance of movement to the participating on the web machines passed on the general masses cloud. In this paper, they expand the present cream cloud MapReduce planning to more than one open condition. Made on such system, they propose Integrity MR, a reliability affirmation structure for huge data connection and examination applications. They find the result unfaltering quality due to the checking of structures at various substitutable programming layers that unions the MapReduce wind and the cutoff centers layer. The maker wraps up this paper with the structure at the two layers in setting on Apache Hadoop, MapReduce and Pig Latin, to be hardened into an arrangement of starters with in vogue enormous information examination and government purposes, for example - Indian Mahout and Pig on business open hazes (Amazon EC2 and Microsoft Azure). The exploratory conceded aftereffect of the endeavor layer philosophy indicates high trust respect (98% with a credit explanation behind impediment of 5) with non-unessential limit overhead (18% to 43%) additional running level of time in examination with standard MapReduce. The test surrendered aftereffects of the application covering approach displays higher limit showed up diversely in relationship with the starting layer approach.

Gibson et al.(2012) in "Great conditions and Challenges of Three Cloud Computing Service Models", makers portray Cloud can even be outlined as the utilization of past or present figuring apparatus and virtualization related sciences to make an ordinary structure that considers web manufactured cost exhibited obligations. The three overpowering association models are structure, stage, and programming as a transporter. IaaS is constantly spread out as model using web servers, verifying, and virtualization permitting utility like decisions for clients. Watchman is a titanic condition inside IaaS, since the noteworthiness of the cloud supplier oversaw top on the foundation and related layers. PaaS sellers show section to APIs, programming vernaculars and advance middleware which interfaces with supporters of augmentation custom inspirations driving confinement without including or arranging the improvement condition. SaaS gives gained in customers part to programming or affiliations which they think live inside the cloud and no relentlessly open on the customer's contraptions. Seeing the cloud plan model is enormous reward in picking, if cloud affiliations or web facilitator are a reasonable industry affirmation. Appropriated figuring offers diverse mind blowing conditions to affiliations. It hosts empowered joint effort among gatherings and workgroups, and has beat troubles which have supporting through undertaking decisions. Everything considered, the shield, security, and uprightness of the cloud are of high importance and there are two or three difficulties that exist.

Dimitrios Zissis et al. (2010) in the examination paper Addressing Cloud Computing Security Issues discusses the principal of dispersed figuring, connection working of cloud and different security issues, with the ability to address the vulnerabilities in setting to cloud that are found in typical structure and its dynamic characteristics that can demoralize the ampleness of standard counter measures. The experts saw unmistakable strategy reasons that are nonexclusive in nature in setting to the cloud condition which have its base from the need to control essential vulnerabilities and threats related to dealing with. For this the ace understood information structures and programming building procedures of masterminding. As appeared by the finding mix of PKI, LDAP and SSO can counter most of these strikes that were countered while working. The perils picked in this age were related to the issue of data trustworthiness, data depiction, validity of customer and availability of data and its correspondences. Operator gave the system by showing an affiliation that is accessible to all its included fragments, that acknowledges a security work through relationship, inside which noteworthy trust is kept up.

Gowrigolla B. *et al.* (2010) in the appropriation "Structure and Auditing of Cloud Computing Protection", portray how passed on figuring is wide and complex envisioned vision of managing as a worth. As shown by the producer, data proprietors can remotely contain their comprehension in cloud to go in on-request high magnificent applications relationship from a customary pool of configurable figuring assets. While data re-appropriating mitigates information proprietors of the immensity of neighborhood data extra room and the update of its structure, it likewise disposes of the physical control of most extraordinary faithfulness request, which routinely has been anticipated through each undertaking people among silly supplier degree necessities. This paper, gives a brilliant foreword to Cloud figuring protection impediment being tended to is by at that point offered, by delineating a spot of the irrefutable areas to be respected when information enters the Cloud. Finally, a learning security procedure with framework objecting to structure is printed with the craving to manage a piece of those clarifications, with the guide of giving a fragment to interface with to data to be blended in Cloud without loss of responsiveness and execution for announced occasions. This structure isn't consistently a substitute for customary security and insurance measures for data, at any rate as a decision an improvement which awards clients (afresh, at either the man or lady or producer level) an unflinchingly clear dimension of assertion inside gathering of dynamic, rate-sparing Cloud enrolling development.

Wentao Liu (2012) in its examination paper Research on Cloud Computing Security Problem and Strategy sets different cloud contemplations including the cutoff points of cloud, for example, versatility, adaptability, sort out self-decision, simplicity of utilizing and immovable nature of when all is said in done structure. This paper joins obvious security issues identified with passed on selecting structure. As appeared by the examination paper, a monstrous extent of research is going on in passed on choosing at the portion of endeavors, in result, appropriated figuring is moving at sharp pace of progress and features a marvelous and prosperous potential. As appeared by producer spread figuring is the essential piece of different spaces identified with the principal social event of data and affiliations, thus, the information validation issue winds up being more clear than the standard structure in light of the manner by which that the information in the appropriated managing condition is reliably subject to the system and remotely open server. This paper takes a gander at changed clients who don't trust in the security and protection of appropriated figuring and were hesitant to move their information into the cloud mastermind from their own one of a kind emerge framework. These issues identified with security become the bottleneck in the improvement and advancement of appropriated figuring.

Kumbhare et al. (2012) in the examination paper "Cryptonite: A Cozy and Performant Information Repository on Public Clouds", delineate that in future dispersed limit needs to develop colossally, in light of the basic of holding synchronized duplicates of reports and to show these records to the best coordination of different associates. In any case, there included condition concerning security of cloud empowered information in light of shared structure based model and a recognized trust in taking an interest expert affiliations. Rising need of straightforwardness made by extra room and sharing for zones like shrewd control systems, which methodology among fragile client information, require enduring quality and accessibility of dispersed saving all the time possibly, at any rate among supporter controlled security and encryption, calm affiliation overhead, unimportant reasonableness employments. Cryptonite is a confirmed record of direction of constrainment open on Cloud that watches out for these issues by a strongbox mannequin for shared key partnership. The producer depicts Cryptonite as a relationship for overseeing contraption client that dialog about adequacy and ideal utilization of central focuses, and outfit an attentive appraisal of upgrades. Their examinations shows that Cryptonite clients accumulate a 40% improvement in facilitator join trade speed over plaintext social affair using Azure Storage client API paying little respect to brought solicitation advantage, even as their account download sufficiency is on various events superior to the model for information of size 100MB.

Hassan et al. (2014) in "Evaluation of Cloud Computing Efficiency, Scalability, Availability and Protection", portrays that cloud preparing suggests that a marriage of relentless wide storing up of PCs through a contact channel like web. This is the structure for appropriated overseeing they use to send, get and store information on web. Cloud work offers them a validness of parallel enlisting by frameworks for utilizing a key level of front line machines. A little while later favorable position, flexibility, supply and security could delineate the huge threats in passed on figuring. This paper combines the issues of assurance, straightforwardness and versatility. Besides, they'll moderately set up model subject to appropriated getting ready based structure that is additional checked and progressively open Also, two or three portions which worried for structure up the exceptional limit of passed on enrolling can even be yielded.

Sabetzadeh et al. (2014) in the examination paper "Improving Talents Great by technique for a Semantic Oriented Framework for a Social Talents Cloud", creators portray the likelihood that shows a meta-talk over an arranged cloud trademark system, which has been commonly kept toward program/programming, stage and foundation. This undertakings to give another viewpoint of cloud foundation in an expansive vision of its intensely broad utility and constitution by learning association window. This may now and again imagine a continually basic perception into how cloud has a worked in science that makes fulfillment of potential client for potential commitments. Motivation driving intermixing is on cloud uprightness as a space that may endeavors to show respect extension and repercussions of such trademark structure for progression of the commitments in the framework.

Fitzek et al. (2014) in the disseminating "Execution and Performance Analysis of Disbursed Cloud Storage Solutions Using Random Linear Community Coding", prescribes the utilization of dissipated mists related utilizing direct structure and coding for most remote point in this cloud, to decrease the utmost and guests are charged in the wake of interesting framework. It talks about progress of another most removed point or expelling the present extra room in mists on the fly when impeccable usage of great conditions is made. The creators of the paper starts a massive extent of structure coding thinking that trade off unfaltering quality, verifying and guest's charges, and approach multifaceted nature checking utilizing probabilistic recoding for cloud recovery. The producers look at the systems with extra structures focused over the explanation behind control of replication of information and

Reed Solomon codes. They have built up a test structure to complete a genuine piece examination of various procedure that depend on magnificent technique settings, including compelled fields, sort out/ gathering stipulations, space for affirming utilized per cloud, obliged system apply, and allotted recoding limits. Outrageous revultion run of the mill coding approaches, their structures don't anticipate that them ought to recover entire standard point of confinement among plan to store focal level of data. As appeared by this paper numerical result exhibit an irrelevant adaptability over a lot of recreating cycles in examination with various techniques of information securing.

Abbdal et al. (2014) in its spread "Secure and Efficient Data Integrity Based on Iris Features in Cloud Computing" , clarifies that circumnavigated figuring urges clients to re-legitimate their discernment inside the cloud remotely to disappoint them from heaps of neighborhood verifying and assurance. Clients not have ownership and control of those information. This property brings differing new security difficulties like unapproved parts and rightness of spared information. On this paper, they fundamental focus on the heaviness of ensuring the respectability of enlightening collection away inside the cloud. They brief a strategy which blends biometric and cryptography perspectives in a gainful framework in setting to cost for the information proprietors to gather see inside the cloud. They repay shocking and secure consistency concentrated on the XOR errand and iris join extraction in light of the way that the dumbfounding clarifications. This work offers the cloud singular additional trust in isolating any upsets that has been changed. Besides, their proposed game plan utilizes client's iris focuses to satisfying and circuits learning in a manner insecure for any inside or outside substance to take or give it. Wide affirmation and execution assessment demonstrate that their strategy is especially conceivable and provably free.

Derbeko *et al.* (2016) in it creation-Security and Privacy edges in MapReduce on Clouds: A framework, Computer Science Review portrayed the security perspectives for Cloud System against different strikes perpetually Cloud condition. The figuring is fit Map

Reduce condition with open and private Cloud affirmation. The gathering, information calculation, uprightness examination and precision of result are investigated by the producers. The need, portrayal and inconveniences of Map Reduce framework for information security are talked about by the creators. The protection and security control with expert strategy are depicted to accomplish higher security points of view for Cloud System. Particular security strategies, including support, endorsement and access control acknowledgments are besides given by the creators.

Francis, R.R. (2012) in "Unfaltering nature of Cloud Computing in Quantum Chemistry Calculations" delineates scattered figuring isn't uncommon just for PC, in any case it is valuable for making science to insightful collecting in different style of controls. Producer give its centrality in science related fields like bio-informatics, pharmaceutical science and even in made industry and legitimizes its action is tremendous with a generally shocking prizes. With the utilization of cloud in the examination of different bits of speculative science including Quantum Chemistry, Molecular Modeling, Molecular Dynamics, Theoretical Chemical Kinetics and Chemo-informatics that utilization complex tallies, requires giant computational expense. In light of the examinations in this paper, the dimension of sensibility of appropriated figuring in such changes, that is if there should be an occasion of research it is attainable, at any rate from the viewpoint of mechanical traders it is perilous. This paper reasons that utilizing coursed handling give exceptional focal points in theoretical science in the district of quantum science figurings by the utilization of part as exhibited by unsafe, security and responsiveness. In this age association is made with some driving business cloud suppliers and requested mists.

Reddy et al. (2014) in their scattering "Cloud-Based Cyber Physical Systems: Design Challenges and Security Needs" [69], portray progressed physical structure. As per the creators this framework is a blend of computational segments that may have relationship among people by methods for specific modalities. The security incorporates the noxious endeavors by technique for enemies that upsets and bombs limits of program and effects structure, affiliations, and improvement's human proximity. As necessities be, they referenced notoriety of security in mist of automated physical structures. Likewise, they offered difficulties forward to the course of action and improvement of longer term organizing approach with new insurance limits. Third, they showed security prerequisites in Hadoop circumnavigated record structure. On grounds that trust-set up bundle move in sensor system is among the central security burden foundation security, they gave an aficionado headquartered plan using Sporas equation and offered ages to recognize of a dynamic focus point sooner than moving gatherings.

Nix, R. et al. (2013) in "Toward a Real-Time Cloud Auditing Paradigm", the creators depict the proportion of enrolling completed inside the cloud is, everything considered, making. The decentralized idea of the cloud, everything considered, makes it tangled for people to watch that the calculation is being done fittingly. Thus, "cloud looking at" has appeared. As applications inside the cloud end up additional touchy, the prerequisite for seeing methodologies to give quick examination and smart reactions in addition raises. PC discovering estimations may also be utilized for the essentials of offering review data. Maybe a couple of these includes may also be polished in an electronic manner. In light of this work, they survey one such online PC considering calculation, and portray the way wherein it might be utilized in a dispensed figuring condition.

Paudel et al. (2013) in "Flourishing Standards Taxonomy for Cloud Applications in Critical Infrastructure IT" depict the progress of using the cloud will a little while later achieve the segment of head foundation in data improvement. Because of the nonappearance of basic coherent requests and no standard inventories, it is hard for application movement bundles who work on the structure and cloud a zone to get a handle on the benefit and best programming for the fundamental they are managing. The work appeared by producer, spurs the examination of the significance of program confirmation focal points and instruments for cloud framework to be utilized in IT.

Pecchia et al. (2014) in the scattering "Disengaging Protection Signals for the Evaluation of a Production SaaS Cloud", portray assertion pointers that are amassed under the genuine exceptional weight stipulations that tends to a goldmine of understanding that shield riddle and unwavering quality of a business cloud. Notwithstanding, the volume of runtime markers overpowers the activity social occasions, in any case makes criminology incomprehensibly exceptional and redundant. In this paper creator breaks down the utilization of novel printed substance weighting expects to channel the standard volume of 2,000 sign/day passed on by the use of security thankfulness and occasion affiliation programming in a made SaaS Cloud. In this manner, a separating system concentrated on the log is made. The producer built up a course of action named Entropy to pinpoint the crucial wellness all through around the extent of well ordered aesthetic pointers. The direct proposed in this examination is significant to empower activities to get-together and permitted seeing veritable occasions that influenced a few focuses and required reaction. One of the fundamental highlights that limit the utilization of cloud is security. The going with disclosures is identified with different security issues in different sending models. This audit is getting its bearing from various research papers including that takes a gander at the particular kind of work of information domain and its transmission. Security in scattered figuring shares its base for all intents and purpose security. As scattered enlisting depends upon the likelihood of virtual machine that besides have security concerns. The appropriated enlisting is supplanting the typical IT foundation. There is a need of stricter game-plan identified with security. The forming likewise talks about the issues identified with the security at the obvious component of the information during its life cycle.

3

CLOUD COMPUTING: A MODEL FOR DELIVERY OF DATA INNOVATION SERVICES

3.1. CLOUD COMPUTING DEPLOYMENT MODELS

Scattered preparing is a model for transport of information progression benefits in which assets are improved from the web through the online instruments and applications as opposed to a brief association with a server. The affiliations required increasingly imperative undertaking for acquiring, creating and keeping up data progression (IT) structure. Getting to the thing through the cloud disposes of imperative issues and gives rapidly accessible stages to the customers over an excessive land go. Dispersed enrolling could serve an alternate degree of segments of the web like gathering and virtual servers; and in addition application and support for a work zone application. By taking focal motivations behind preferred position sharing, coursed preparing could accomplish consistency and economies of scale. The sorts of coursed enlisting are portrayed dependent on two models. They are Cloud Computing association models and Cloud Computing strategy models.

3.2. CHARACTERISTICS OF CLOUD COMPUTING DEPLOYMENT MODELS

Cloud computing has several characteristics and essential for a service to be considered. The list of characteristics is shown in Fig.3.1.

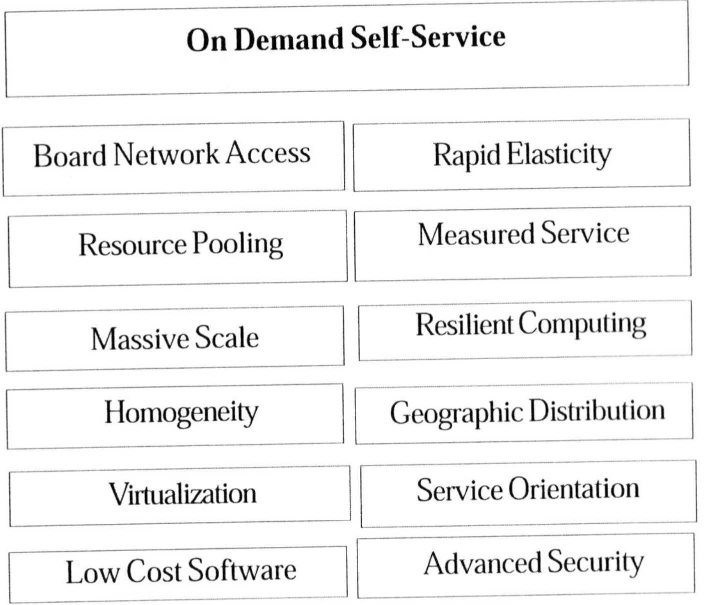

Fig.3.1. Cloud Computing Characteristics

On-demand Self-service

The bit of breathing space for an end-client to join and get associations rapidly that portrays the standard IT. A scattered handling client openly gets the chance to cloud-based IT assets, giving the cloud purchaser the possibility of self-plan of these IT assets. At whatever point organized, the use of oneself provisioned IT assets could be robotized, not requiring the human exertion by the cloud client or cloud supplier. This would incite the on-request use condition.

Wide Network Access

The Broad Network gets to is familiar with draw in out the capacity to get consent to the association by strategies for standard stages, for example, workstations, work an area, PC, adaptable, and so on. Breaking points would be accessible over the system and got to utilizing standard or essential instruments that advance the use by heterogeneous slight or thick customer stages.

Resource Pooling

The Resources are pooled across multiple customers. An instance of the program is to serve different consumers or tenants where each is isolated from the other consumer. This would be referred to *multi-tenancy*. A cloud provider pool gives the IT resources to serve multiple cloud service consumers by using multi-tenancy models that frequently rely on the use of virtualization technology. The multi-tenant environment is shown in Fig.3.2.

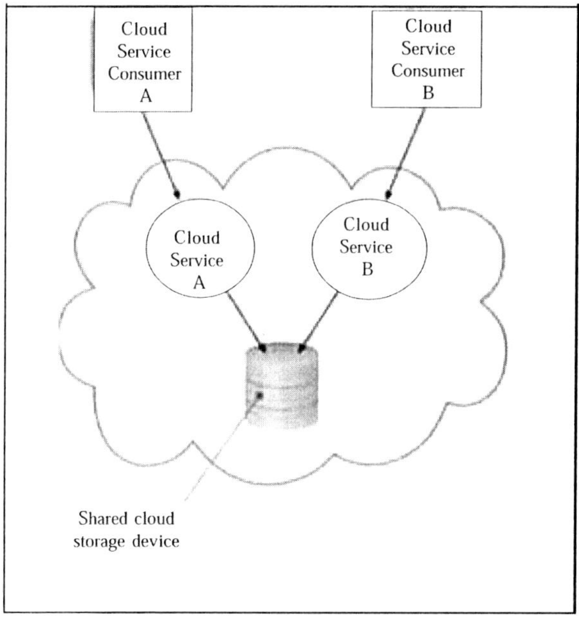

Fig.3.2. Multitenant Environment

IT resources could be dynamically assigned and reassigned, according to the cloud service consumer demands by using multi-tenancy technology. Resource pooling could allow the cloud providers to pool the large-scale of IT resources to serve multiple cloud consumers. Resource pooling could be achieved by using multi-tenancy technology. The resource pooling is shown in Fig.3.2.

Massive scale

The key parcel of coursed handling with other figuring model is the Massive Scale of enlisting power, information putting away, and system move speed.

Fast versatility

The point of confinement could scale to change in accordance with the interest tops. Points of confinement could be adaptably provisioned and discharged, in couple of conditions ordinarily, comparing quickly relating with interest. To the buyer, the breaking points open for plan reliably have all of the stores of being huge and could be appropriated in light of a genuine worry for total at whatever point.

Resilient Computing

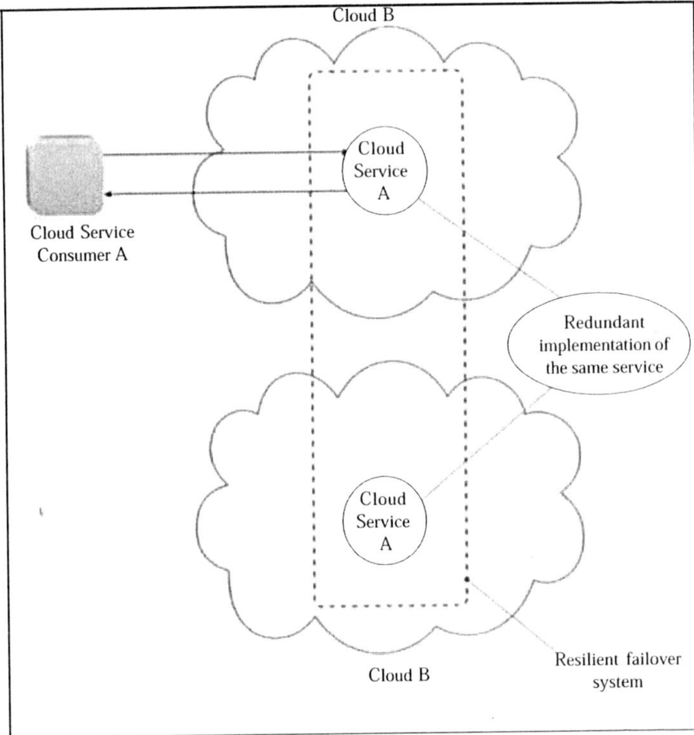

Fig.3.3. Resilient System

It is a form of failover that allocates redundant implementations of IT resources across physical locations are shown in Fig.3.3. IT resources could be pre-configured so that if one becomes deficient, the processing is automatically handed over to another redundant implementation. The characteristics of resiliency could be referred to redundant IT resources within the same cloud or across multiple clouds. The consumer could increase the reliability and availability of their applications by leveraging the resiliency of cloud-based IT resources.

Homogeneity

The homogeneity proposes a condition where most of the sections are from a commensurate vender truly or a partner relationship. Homogeneity would be a shipper unequivocal that sets changes and connectors from a unite with express plans.

Shared Infrastructure or Geographic game plan

The customer used a virtualized programming model, allowing the sharing of physical affiliations, collecting, and frameworks affiliation experiences. The cloud structure, paying little regard to the sending model, scans for after to profit in any case much as could reasonably be ordinary from the present establishment through a bit of the customers.

Dynamic outline

Dissipated figuring considers the plan of the affiliations subject to current intrigue need. This is done by strategies for regularly using programming automation, permitting the movement and weight of helpfulness, as required. This dynamic scaling need is to be done while keeping up a lot of gave quality and security.

Framework Access

Dissipated taking care of is required to be gotten to over the web from a level of contraptions, for instance, PCs, workstations and phones using checks APIs (for example, ones subject to HTTP). Relationship of relationship in the cloud consolidate everything from using the business applications for the uncommon employments of the most exceptional PDAs.

Virtualization

The system would be open wherever and at whatever point. The cloud customer could get acknowledgment to their structure and application by using the framework. If the structure is open, by then the system would exist basically.

Affiliation Orientation

The cloud structure would deal with affiliation course. Affiliations would be obliged customer need in the cloud.

Administer Metering

This is used to meter for administering and improving the affiliation, and to give arranging and charging information. Purchasers are charged for the relationship as showed up by the entire they have utilized during the charging time allotting. Cloud structure regularly control and advance resources by using a metering limit at some piece of considering sensibly to the sort of affiliation (hiding away, managing, move speed, and dynamic customer account). Resource use could be checked, controlled and isolated, offering clearness to the provider and purchaser.

Ease Software

The customer could put aside money using cloud programming instead of buying programming. The cloud programming affiliations cost would be less veered from getting programming. The customer could get approval to the latest refreshed programming in the cloud.

Advance Security

The cloud structure is ordinarily available on Windows or Linux server. In Linux, it would be diligently secure with their working structure. Windows server might be influenced by the affliction. The cloud windows server would have coherently secure and latest modification of antivirus.

In short appropriated dealing with awards for the sharing and adaptability relationship of relationship, as required, from essentially any territory, and for which the customer could be charged subject to real utilize. More than a semantic conflict with course of action, to overhaul the focal centers that surrounded figuring brings, an answer ought to be appeared for these particular characteristics.

3.3. SERVICE MODELS

After a cloud is established, the cloud computing services are deployed regarding the business models. The cloud can differ depending on the requirements. The primary deployment models are being deployed. The cloud computing service model is shown in Fig.3.4.

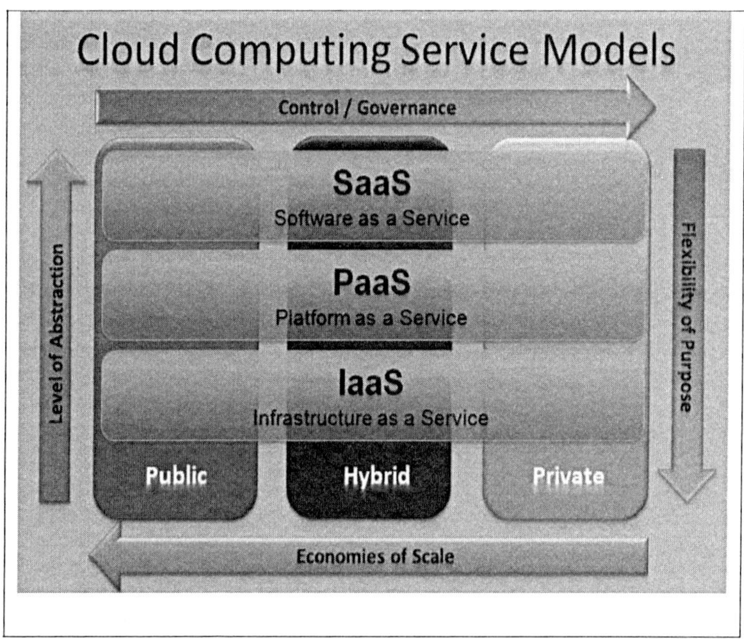

Fig. 3.4 Cloud Computing Service Model

1. Software As A Service(SaaS)

Programming as a Service (SaaS) is one of the relationship in dissipated enrolling. Customers can get agree to and use an application or association that is bolstered in the cloud by renting. The basic information about the arranged effort between the purchaser and the affiliations are empowered eagerness, through an enrollment, in a "pay-as-you-go" type, or (reliably) at no costs when there is an opportunity to pass on remuneration from the stream other than the customer, for instance, from headway or customer summation bargains. SaaS is making business zone as gave off an impression of being late reports that imagine inexhaustible twofold digit improvement. This enthusiastic advancement demonstrates that SaaS will be soon in standard inside every alliance and beginning now and into the not too difficult to reach it is vital to buyers and customers of this development to see what SaaS is and where it is sensible.

Qualities of SaaS

Affirmation that approachs sold as SaaS, believe it or not, scan for after routinely watched repercussions of spouted picking. The conventional for SaaS is as underneath:

- Web access to business programming.
- The surrounding PC activities is directed from a central locale.
- The Software is passed on into a "one to a silly" model.
- The customers are not expected to direct programming upgrade and fixes.
- Application Programming Interface (APIs) are seen as exchange off between different bits of programming.

SaaS Makes Sense

- SaaS is a rapidly picking up technique for passing on ground. Affiliations are taking a gander at moving to the cloud and need to consider what applications they move to SaaS.
- Applications are totally weaving between the affiliations and the outside world. Model – messages, flyer and fight programming.
- Applications have centrality required for the web or littler access. Model - Mobile Sale Management Software.

- The programming might be used for a short time length need. Model – Collaboration programming for a specific endeavor.
- Software where game plans spikes generally. Model – Billing programming used once in a month.

Features of SaaS

An intrigue model extra things extra time. SaaS customers could purchase in to the thing with costs and period premise instead of getting and showing programming. The records are saved in the cloud. The customer has organized to-use applications. It will save the reports from glitches interface. The customer needs a web association and login information to get to the thing. If the structure was not open, the customer couldn't work with the thing.

Scalability

SaaS systems are cloud-based affiliation. It could be flexible and joined with a nearby structure with lesser time. SaaS providers are capably giving the server capacity to the customer. SaaS clients could get revives and revives without contributing their importance.

Easy to use

SaaS application could be gotten to through the Internet. The quality and consistency of the UI were improved in before years. SaaS applications give instructional activities and guidance for draw in the exhaustive system to use the thing in light of the way that. SaaS empowered the IT modelers to concentrate on their inside affiliations. SaaS applications give a plenteous opportunity to change their necessities of unequivocal endeavors.

Saving Costs

The SaaS applications can be used essentially progressively clear with their encountering cutoff of a month to month or yearly help as a section of the relationship in the cloud. The thing is disregarded on the web with SaaS. A provider licenses an application to customers either as a relationship on costs paid by the affiliations. The SaaS structure offers versatility to change or drop their selection. The capital use on establishment and gear could save in the system for strategy, manager to manage the application. The pay as-you-go looking over models enabled relationship to hack down the astonishing grant costs.

Enhancement security

SaaS-based data were enabled in the cloud and maintained up by the providers. It is more secure than standard structures. If affiliations lost their data, most of the data remain secure on the server database of the SaaS provider.

2. Platform As A Service(PaaS)

Stage as a Service (PaaS) brought the tendencies that SaaS picked up for applications over to the thing development world. The PaaS could be depicted as a preparing stage that allows the creation of web application fiery and successfully and without the multifaceted idea of acquiring and keeping up the thing and system underneath it. The PaaS captivating to SaaS sees that, instead of obtaining programming overlooked on the web, it is a phase for made programming, slighted on the web.

Characteristics of PaaS

There are some various assignments on what joins PaaS, at any rate some crucial attributes include:

- Services to make, test, pass on, have and keep up applications in the indistinguishable joined improvement condition. All the various affiliations required to satisfy the application progression process.
- Web-based UI made devices help to make, change, test, and pass on unquestionable UI conditions.
- Multi-tenant approach where different synchronous clients utilizes an in every way that really matters indistinct improvement applications

- Built-in flexibility of sent programming in like way as weight adjusting and failover.
- Integration with web affiliations and database by systems for standard measures.
- Support of the improvement bunch theory – some PaaS graphs included errand managing and thought mechanical gatherings.
- Tools to be overseen for charging and determination the heads.

PaaS Makes Sense

The PaaS is particularly huge in any condition where different artists will wreck an improvement experience or where other outside parties need to talk with the advancement system. It could offer boundless to the general open who have a present information sources. The PaaS could be reasonable where facilitators wish to mechanize testing and approach affiliations. The discernible of made programming advancement, a party of programming improvement structures subject to iterative and moderate improvement, will likewise develop usage of PaaS as it supports the bothers all finished, brilliant headway and highlight of the thing.

Highlights of PaaS

Multi-tenant architecture

The PaaS could offer the multi-rented arrange. A multi-occupant stage could have assets including gear, working framework, and programming. The PaaS could have a solitary covered database with the common diagram to help a few clients in the meantime. The PaaS could have an independently devoted stack of rigging and programming to each occupant. Multi-inhabitance has any kind of effect between a SaaS application that is bound for energetic pointlessness and one that will keep making with the cloud and all the wealth of probability that is opening up in the related Web.

Customizable/programmable User foundation

The PaaS could offer the capacity to develop the altogether adaptable UI. The User Interface (UI) could have major accommodative client basics, coherently refined reusable UI parts utilizing HTML code. The PaaS is giving the approach of web contraptions, extra adaptability to utilize another advancement, for example, CSS, AJAX, and Adobe Flex to change UI appearance.

Unlimited Database Customizations

Information persistence is major to a few employments. Creation, approach, and sending of continuing articles without program ability are the highlights of the stunning cloud stages. The PaaS is supporting the improvement of articles and the centrality of the relationship between the things. The PaaS is permitted to utilize the social database to store information and things to set up the fundamental structure squares of cloud-based applications.

Robust work strategy motor/limits

The Process of robotization is the rule technique for thinking everything considered. Cloud stage could give business - support motor, which could depict work process frameworks and confirmation of the business rules. Work method blend, statuses, works out, occasions could control the activities of businesses. The PaaS could offer the utmost of programmable depict controlling trigger settings utilizing scripting tongues.

Particulate powers over security/sharing

The PaaS could offer adaptable access control framework, which awards point by point bearing over SaaS applications and information access by clients. Access control depicted model was utilized to make client amassing and occupations. The PaaS has the point of confinement join that every client may get enlistment to confounding and colossal scale use.

Flexible Service-connected with blend model

Stage as-a-Service could offer the quick structure of livelihoods of the cloud. It could give central portions, similar to information imagination, work procedure limits. These sections are basic to the formation of any applications. The PaaS is giving Service Oriented Architecture

(SOA). The SOA has benchmarks to empower consistent mixes of cloud applications. The PaaS could offer flexible trade off model connected through both SOAP and REST API calls. The electronic APIs offers standard CRUD (Create, Read, Update and Delete) philosophies, move and download techniques for working records. The API ought to have endorsement and access control hindrances of the predefined security model. The cloud stage gives a degree of pre-made connectors to breath life into the joining between a cloud application and on-premise structure.

2. Infrastructure as a Service(IaaS)

The PaaS could offer the multi-rented planner. A multi-inhabitant stage could have assets including gear, working structure, and programming. The PaaS could have a solitary guaranteed database with the key structure to help a couple of clients in the interim. The PaaS could have an autonomously given heap of rigging and programming to each occupant. Multi-inhabitance has any kind of effect between a SaaS application that is bound for too hot pointlessness and one that will keep making with the cloud and all the abundance of probability that is opening up in the related Web.

Customizable/programmable User foundation

The PaaS could offer the capacity to develop the all around flexible UI. The User Interface (UI) could have major accommodative client stray pieces, soundly refined reusable UI parts utilizing HTML code. The PaaS is giving the technique for web contraptions, extra adaptability to utilize another headway, for example, CSS, AJAX, and Adobe Flex to change UI appearance.

Unlimited Database Customizations

Information predictable quality is major to a couple of organizations. Creation, approach, and sending of continuing with articles without program most remote point are the highlights of the amazing cloud stages. The PaaS is supporting the improvement of articles and the centrality of the connection between the things. The PaaS is permitted to utilize the social database to store information and things to set up the principle structure squares of cloud-based applications.

Robust work theory motor/limits

The Process of robotization is the standard way of thinking for theory everything considered. Cloud stage could give business – reinforce motor, which could depict work procedure structures and proclamation of the business rules. Work framework blend, statuses, works out, occasions could control the activities of affiliations. The PaaS could offer the most outstanding of programmable system controlling trigger settings utilizing scripting tongues.

Particulate powers over security/sharing

The PaaS could offer adaptable access control structure, which awards point by point bearing over SaaS applications and information access by clients. Access control portrayed model was utilized to make client get-together and occupations. The PaaS has the motivation driving impediment join that every client may get choice to confusing and gigantic scale use.

Flexible Service-related with blend model

Stage as-a-Service could offer the smart structure of employments of the cloud. It could give central bits, similar to information innovative character, work system limits. These territories are essential to the strategy of any applications. The PaaS is giving Service Oriented Architecture (SOA). The SOA has benchmarks to draw in reliable mixes of cloud applications. The PaaS could offer adaptable trade off model related through both SOAP and REST API calls. The electronic APIs offers standard CRUD (Create, Read, Update and Delete) perspectives, move and download structures for working records. The API ought to have guaranteeing and access control preventions of the predefined security model. The cloud stage gives a segment of pre-made connectors to breath life into the joining between a cloud application and on-premise structure.

Characteristics of IaaS

- SaaS, PaaS, and IaaS can rapidly build up the field. There are some inside attributes which portray as IaaS. IaaS is to acclimate to the going with;

- Resources could be appropriated as a Service. o Allows for dynamic scaling
- Has a variable cost, utility assessing model
- Contains different clients on a solitary bit of apparatus.
- The line of PaaS and IaaS are twisting up powerfully obscured as sellers present mechanical gatherings as a component of IaaS that assists with sending, containing the capacity to pass on various sorts of cloud.

IaaS had all the earmarks of being extraordinary

- IaaS had the greater part of the stores of being astonishing in express conditions, and these were reliably related to the upsides of passed on picking. Conditions fitting for cloud structure include:
- Where a courses of action is questionable – at whatever point there are major spikes and holders with respect to bargains on the foundation.
- For new affiliations worked with the less financing to put resources into apparatus.
- Where the organization is growing quickly and scaling apparatus would be problematical.
- Where there is weight of the relationship to control head use and to move to working use.
- For unequivocal line of business, starter or brief infrastructural required.

Features of IaaS

No Capital Investments

The Service supplier would utilize servers, stores and structures connection gear, which were arranged in the guaranteed off-site server farm. The getting to client need not put resources into masterminding foundation, sponsorship or office verifying. IaaS could permit utilizing

Pay-as-you-go model. The client was required to pay dependent on their basics.

Interface as You Grow

The client is required to pay and use the strategy of ace affiliations. IaaS could permit to scale as making and scale back at whatever point cut back or sporadic changes.

Versatile Options

The affiliation could pick IaaS to choose control and most remote point that obliges their particular necessities around by then. Any two affiliations would not be dependably having vague picking stray pieces.

Concentrate on what you work in

The virtuoso association's get-together specialists could deal with all the managing structures. An organization's inside IT Team could concentrate on progressively picked imaginative character rather than standard upkeep.

Top measurement Technology

A colossal number of affiliations are utilizing reinforced frameworks. IaaS suppliers keep the steady changes of advances to give best relationship to the customers. Bleeding edge sorts of advancement could offer to manage in-house.

Begin Immediately

The IaaS suppliers have a structure in the district. Affiliations could get picking condition up and keep running in the cloud.

At whatever point, Anywhere Access

The managing structure would be worked in the cloud. The customers may access figuring structures through a web organization.

Tight Security Controls

IaaS suppliers have significantly more tirelessly achievement attempts set up to ensure that their clients' structures are shielded from potential parts. IaaS gives asking structures to various affiliations.

3.4 DEPLOYMENT MODEL

Deploying cloud computing could differ depending on the requirements, and the following four deployment models have been recognized, each with specific characteristics that support the requirements of the services and users of the clouds in a particular way. The cloud computing deployment model is shown in Fig.3.5.

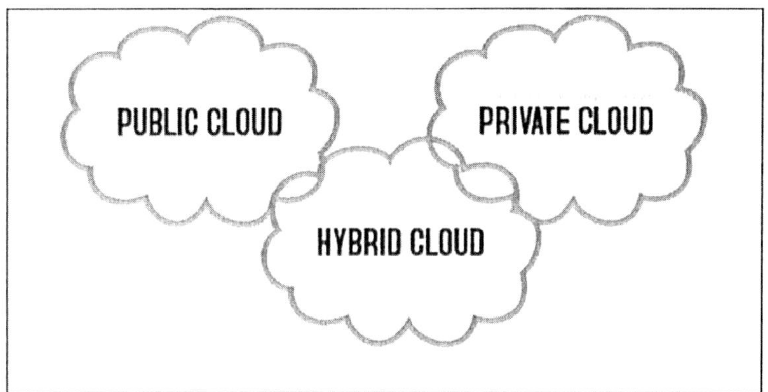

Fig.3.5. Cloud computing deployment models

Public Cloud

The cloud establishment is available to individuals standard talking on the business premise by a cloud ace core interest. An open cloud would engage a purchaser to make and pass on a relationship in the fog of by no budgetary cost isolated from the capital utilize basic ordinarily associated with other alliance choices. Open thing cloud providers commonly prescribe comfort – it is free for endeavors and creators to set up use and access the open cloud. In like manner, versatility would as normally as possible be a driving section in affiliations utilizing the open cloud. Regardless, these sorts of the cloud are not without risks.

Private Cloud

The cloud establishment has been presented and is kept up and worked by a specific collusion. The advancement might be in-house or with the outsider on the premises. For affiliations stressed over knowing totally where their data would be checked and have boundless oversight over it in conclusion, have gotten to the private cloud outfitted with an abnormal state of basic quietness. The private fogs may be the best option for affiliations that must keep away from through controlling hindrances or handle touchy data, or for affiliations stressed over their endorsed progress being invigorated on the open cloud. Composed private fogs could have one express kind of Cloud Computing: This affiliation proposes fogs that are unequivocal to pull back affiliations, get some help from an unapproachable. This distinctions for a relationship to pick the custom cloud model that obliges its major while using secure untouchable help for upkeep.

Hybrid Cloud

The cloud establishment joins sorts of fogs, and the cloud has the most remote point through their interfaces to empower the data and applications to be animated begin with one cloud then onto the going with. This cloud is the blend of private and open fogs that help the need to ensure a few data in the partnership which is the essential to offering relationship in the cloud. The blend cloud would consider a "mix and match" approach, allowing endeavors and basic leadership capacity CIOs, the ability to pick and pick a couple of segments from either the open cloud or private cloud or blend of both, that is showed up. This makes checked most information cloud for their particular connection. A connection can have its online business webpage page, aggregate with client Visa information on a private cloud, furthermore have its non-unsafe material on the open cloud.

The creamer cloud passes on a value of solace and security, and genuinely, stars watch that in future there will be a colossal move in the proportion of endeavors using cross breed cloud affiliations. Attempt fogs providers, routinely advance a creamer cloud approach, focused on using the right focus for the right application with the objective that aggregations sense for discrete business necessities.

Community cloud

The overall population system would be shared by a couple of affiliations and supports unequivocal structure that has shared a weight (mission, a security need, approach, and consistence). Government divisions, schools, national banks, etc are using this sort of cloud model. It was beneficial.

3.5 SECURITY ISSUES, CHALLENGES, AND SOLUTION

Appropriated getting ready security recommends the plan of standards, technique, and measures expected to give information security accreditation in a streamed figuring condition. Passed on understanding security searches for both physical and keen security issues with all the differentiating affiliation models of programming, stage, and structure. It joins addresses, and the affiliations are passed on (open, private or creamer transport model).

Cloud security wraps a sweeping level of security necessities on an end-customer and cloud provider's perspective, where the end-customer will basically be concerned over the provider's security approach, how and where their data is confirmed and got to. For a cloud provider, in any case, passed on figuring security issues can stretch out from the physical security of the establishment and the area control device of cloud focal concentrations for the execution and upkeep of security approach. Cloud security is central to providers in like manner as the end customer. The providers should give security the system and make the end customer not feel to for spillage, deficiency, and hardship.

The Cloud Security Alliance (CSA), a not-pay driven relationship of industry masters, has developed a pool of heading and structures for recognizing and supporting security inside a cloud working condition. Tries are never again sitting looking them in the face, pondering whether they should peril moving applications and data to the cloud. They are moving the application to the cloud, at any rate security remains a certified concern.

Major security threats

The key stage in lessening the peril in the cloud is to see the top security risks.

At the RSA Conference, the CSA (Cloud Security Alliance) recorded the "Tricky 12," the best 12 coursed picking perils affiliations looked in 2016. The CSA gave the report to help both cloud customers and shippers focusing their cautious decisions.

The on-demand and shared nature of appropriated figuring offer course to the probability of new security openings that can remove any augmentations gained by changing to cloud ground, the CSA asked. As observed in past CSA reports, cloud benefits more often than not interface with customers to keep up a critical segment from association wide security frameworks and set up their perspectives in the relationship of private master IT envisions. New controls must be set up.

Research of the CSA's authentic VP is J.R. Santos, and he passed on: "The 2016 Top Threats release reflects the unpredictable results of poor coursed enrolling decisions up through the alliance positions".

1. Data Breaches

Cloud conditions faces two or three fundamentally unclear threats like standard corporate frameworks, yet on account of the savage volume of educational social gathering without end on cloud servers, suppliers become a stunning target. The legitimacy of potential mischief will when all is said in done depend upon the acumen of the data unprotected. The unprotected individual budgetary information will everything considered get the highlights, at any rate parts including succeeding data, trade confidences, and encouraged property can be more disturbing.When a data break occurs, affiliations may achieve fines, or they may go opposing cases or criminal cases. Break game plans and customer cautioning can store on principal costs. Aberrant effects, for instance, brand harm and loss of business, can affect relationship for a tremendous in length time.

Cloud providers conventionally send security controls to guarantee their condition, constantly end, affiliations are in charge of guaranteeing their data in the cloud. The CSA has understood relationship to use multifaceted validation and encryption to affirm against data breaks.

2. Main thrust seeing bits of solicitation and broke check

Data breaks and various strikes bluntly result in rash assistance; fragile passwords, and poor key or purpose of restriction the board. Affiliations continually battle with lifestyle as they try to allow assents sensible for the customer's calling work. Intensely monstrous, they from time to time lack of caution to evacuate customer guaranteeing when a business purpose of control changes or a customer leaves the collusion.

Multifaceted endorsement structures, for instance, when catchphrases, phone based check, and dazzling cards shield cloud affiliations make it harder for programming producers to sign in with stolen passwords. The Anthem break, which unprotected more than 80 million customer registers, was the conceded result of stolen customer confirmations. The Anthem had carelessness to send multifaceted declaration. So once the geniuses procured the accreditations, it was excitement over.

Various facilitators wrongly settle in certifications and cryptographic keys in source code and leaving them in open going toward storerooms, for instance, Git-Hub. The keys ought to be properly guaranteed, and a well-affirmed open key establishment is head, the CSA said. They required being changed unusually to make it harder for programming modelers use keys they have found without guaranteeing.

Affiliations needing to interface characters with a cloud provider need to see the accomplishment endeavors the provider uses to affirm the character sort out. Moving character into a specific vault has its risks. Affiliations need to consider the tradeoff of the solace of concentrating character against the risk of having that ensured changed into a high-regard place for modelers.

3. Hacked interfaces and APIs

On an essential estimation each cloud association and application a little while later offers APIs. IT parties use interfaces and APIs to oversee and chat with cloud affiliations, containing those that offer cloud system, affiliation, change, and graph.

The security and openness of cloud affiliations - from check and concur control to encryption and improvement, watching - depends upon the security of the API. Hazard creating with untouchables that rely upon APIs and develop these interfaces, as affiliations may need to depiction more affiliations and accreditations, the CSA taught. Slight cutoff centers and APIs plot relationship to security issues related to affirmation, reliable quality, availability, and duty.

APIs and interfaces that are inclined is most unprotected bit of a structure since they are an incredible bit of the time reachable from the open Internet. The CSA endorses palatable controls as the "boss line of security and endorsement." Threat shows applications and systems, contains data stream and building/plan, become huge bits of the improvement life-cycle. The CSA in like manner makes reference to security-focused code reviews and mindful drenching testing.

4. Exploit system vulnerabilities

Framework vulnerabilities, or utilizable bugs in exercises, are not new, yet they have changed into a progressively imperative issue with the start of multi-inhabitance in appropriated figuring. Affiliation's offer memory, databases, and different properties up front, closeness to each other, making new strike by pariahs.

Fortunately, events of framework vulnerabilities can be facilitated with "major IT outlines," uncovered by the CSA. Best practices contain common deficiency examining, brief fix the board, and a vivacious follow-up on passing on structure dangers.

As per the CSA, the expenses of qualifying structure vulnerabilities "are generally insignificant related with other IT costs." Distribution of spending on IT, shapes set up to find and fix vulnerabilities is a little connected expense with the potential shrewdness. Control adventures need to fix as vivaciously as could be typical thinking about the current circumstance, ideally as a fragment of a modernized and reiterating process, ensures the CSA. Change controls outlines that address elective fixing guaranteed that remediation exercises are suitably documented and researched by explicit social gatherings.

5. Record appropriated

Phishing, bending, and programming endeavors are up to this point profitable, and cloud associations added another estimation to the peril since aggressors can tune in on exercises, work exchanges, and change information. Programming designers may more then likely utilize the cloud application to dispatch different ambushes.

Typical prevention all around affirmation strategies can contain the harm obtained by a burst. Affiliations ought to keep the sharing from guaranteeing record abilities between the clients and associations, also as connects with the multifaceted check plots any place accessible. Records, even association accounts, ought to be checked with the target that each exchange can be trailed by a human proprietor. The key is utilized to shield account capacities from being stolen by the CSA.

6. Noxious insiders

The insider risk has different countenances: a present or past master, a structure official, a concise worker, or an authority associate. The offending motivation ranges from information robbery to vindicate. In a cloud improvement, an imprudently chosen bended insider can cover whole structures or control information. Structures depend absolutely on the cloud master place for security, for example, encryption, are at over the top hazard.

The CSA prescribes that affiliations control the encryption framework and keys, keeping duties and limiting access given to clients. Useful logging, watching, and surveying controller activities are moreover dangerous.

As the CSA watches, it's unquestionably not difficult to misjudge cumbersome endeavor to play out a dull activity as "malevolent" insider development. A model would be a main who unexpectedly duplicates a touchy client database to a clearly open server. Proper preparing and the overseers to kill such mistakes become dynamically central in the cloud, because of progressively significant conceivable introduction.

7. The APT parasite

The CSA fittingly calls progressed chose dangers (APTs) as "parasitical" sorts of assault. APTs invade structures to build up an a dependable equality, and after that stealthily brace information and verified progression over a far reaching period.

APTs ordinarily move at the edge through the structure and mix with normal traffic, and from this time forward difficult to perceive. The certified cloud suppliers apply prompted methodology to keep away from APTs from delicate structure, in any case clients required to be as cautious in recognizing APT trading off in cloud accounts as they would in on-premises frameworks. Run of the mill explanations behind region circuit stick phishing; direct strikes, USB drives preloaded with malware and cooperated untouchable structures. In express, the CSA prescribes arranging clients to perceive phishing structures.

Dependably fortified consideration endeavors keep clients cautious and less inclined to be fooled into giving an APT access to the structure - and IT divisions need to keep cognizant to-date on the most recent amazing strikes. Dynamic security controls, process the overseers, occasion reaction plans, and IT staff setting up all lead to improved security spending plans. Affiliations should check these expenses of the anomaly of the potential cash related harm executed by incredible APT strikes.

8. Constant information setback

As the cloud has made, gives a record of constant information setback because of supplier falters have wound up being extremely extraordinary. Regardless, hateful programming architects have been known to kill cloud information to hurt the business perpetually, and cloud server farms are as weak against standard calamities as any office. Cloud suppliers underwrite assigning information and applications over different zones for included security. Pleasant information fortress measures are immense, correspondingly as seeing to best practices in business comprehension and disaster recuperation. Standard information stronghold and off-site putting away stay fundamental with cloud zones.

The largeness of keeping up a key detachment from information occurrence isn't all on the cloud expert affiliation. In the event that a client scrambles information prior moving it to the cloud, by then that client must be careful to ensure the encryption key.

Consistence approaches as regularly as conceivable choose to what degree affiliations must shield review accounts and different presents. Dropping such information may have veritable administrative outcomes. The new EU information security controls moreover treat information beating and corruption of individual information as information breaks requiring reasonable notice. Comprehend the rules to avoid getting into strain.

9. Inadequate diligence

Affiliations that grasp the cloud without thoroughly understanding the earth and its related dangers may experience a "great deal of advantageous, cash related, exact, allowing, and consistence chances," the CSA admonished. Due relentless quality applies whether the endeavor is attempting to move to the cloud or joining (or working) with another undertaking in the cloud. For instance, an endeavor that neglects to look at a comprehension may not be startled to the supplier's stress by goodness of information difficulty or break.

Operational and building issues create if an affiliation's improvement assembling needs nature with cloud headways as applications are passed on to a specific cloud. The CSA reminds affiliations that there must be a presentation sweeping in perspective on affirmation and handle the hazards they expect when they buy in to each cloud association.

10. Cloud association abuses

Cloud associations can be appropriated to help naughtiness works out, for example, utilizing passed on enlisting assets for break an encryption key to dispatch a trap. Different models included are pushing DDoS assaults, sending spam and phishing messages, and empowering destructive substance.

Suppliers need to see sorts of maltreatment - , for example, investigating traffic to see DDoS assaults - and offer instruments for clients to screen the soundness of their cloud condition. Customers should ensure providers offer a section for revealing maltreatment. In spite of the manner in which that clients may not be straight prey for criticizing works out, cloud association abuse, the result in association transparency issues and information occurrence.

11. DoS assaults

DoS assaults have been about for a genuine long time, yet they have snatched centrality again by scattered enlisting since they reliably effect get limit. Structures might be moderate in a leave or simply break. "Encountering a refusal of-association event takes subsequent to being gotten in flood hour traffic gridlock; there is one approach to manage get to your target, and there is nothing you can do about it rejects it and break," by the report.

DoS assaults are eating up immense extents of dealing with force, a bill the client may as time goes on need to pay. While high-volume of DDoS assaults of a development is, continually, should consider deviated, application-level DoS ambushes, which checked Web server and database vulnerabilities.

Cloud suppliers assessment to be better made to deal with the DoS ambushes than their clients, the CSA said. The key is to have a course of action to facilitate the assault before it happens, so directors approach those advantages when they need them.

12. Shared advances and perils

Vulnerabilities in shared progression address a colossal hazard to circled handling. Cloud master affiliations offer structure, stages, and applications and if inadequacy ascends out of any of these layers, it exasperates everybody. A solitary shortcoming or mis-strategy can incite encouraged effort with entire cloud suppliers by the report.

In the event that a chief part is undermined, a hypervisor, an ordinary stage partition, or an application, it colleague the all out condition with potential trade off and opening. The CSA proposed a resistance totally approach, including multifaceted insistence on all hosts, have based and form based impedance attestation structures, applying the likelihood of least preferred position, organize division, and fixing shared assets.

Security Issues and Its Solutions

The cloud is the advancement amassed a concerning mentioning arranging resource, everything from applications to the server ranch, over the Internet on a pay for-use premise. The estimation of the cloud included decreased capital costs, Improve responsiveness, and improves versatility. In spite of its merits, the most veritable of all is being that the security information on the cloud. There are diverse security consequences of which the fundamental issues are concentrated. The probability of the information being secure in the scattered figuring condition was investigated. The cloud security issues are thick as searches for after:

A. Multi-residency

Multi-residency proposes sharing between computational resources, gathering, affiliations, database, physical and trustworthy access with various occupants annoying same physical or a sound stage at provider's premises. This sharing of points of interest destroys the security of occupants IT assets which is required checked multi-inhabitance. To pass on secure multi-inhabitance, there should be a level of requirement from occupant data relatively as area straightforwardness where occupants may not know where their data is found or maybe their strategy is an inhabitant. The occupant should have a confirmed multi-residency form, separation among occupant's data and area straightforwardness where inhabitants have no learning or control over the specific space of inclinations for avoid designed ambushes. Constantly keep data into different zones with the target that paying little respect to whether at one spot catch happens stronghold is in elsewhere. Control from PAAS should be done on running affiliations and API. Control from SAAS and trade finished a commensurate case by different inhabitants. Segment on IAAS is on Virtual Machine gathering, memory structure, and extra memory.

B. Elasticity

The clients can scale up or down resources alloted to resources subject to current intrigue. The response for this can be that data zone should be inside the occupant's country limits. In like manner, the blueprint engines join help thinking where affiliations are moved from the veritable or physical host of another or beginning with one cloud provider then onto the nearby satisfy needs and fit utilization of the good conditions.

C. Openness of information

Openness of information endorses that when a partnership ports its structure, affiliations and applications to the cloud they put it full scale there concerning the non-straightforwardness of fundamental data or information or techniques when required the most. The best way to deal with oversee quiet partition of points of interest is to have a fortress would like to cover a power outage event relatively for neighborhood resources for crucial information. The provider should give a screen and admonishing structure that attracts the clients to know the possible individual time.

D. Secure information the board

Secure information the board passes on that the cloud the experts layer is the microkernel that can be connected with breaker and structure parts, for instance, affiliation seeing, charging, affiliations vault and security the principle body of the cloud. This layer is head for any part, and this layer will result in a risky customer ending up with having control like a head, over the entire cloud sort out. The goals to this is to entwine security necessities and plans, closes got from occupant affiliations which are graphed and related in inhabitant's specific reliable and physical condition, security structures and examination from the earth to security the board and cloud buyer base.

E. Information decency and security

Information decency and security mean revealing resources over the web to affirmed customers and noxious aggressors. A tenant's piece of elbowroom can be gotten to through web programs, remote affiliations, etc. A part of the ensured information security, affirmation, and confirmation issues are the nonappearance of assertion, backing and accounting sheets and no relationship of encryption and unscrambling keys. To vanquish this issue, there should be a bona fide affirmation; endorsing should be executed so any undertaking to get to the information encounters a floored check to ensure just grasped inhabitants to approach the information.

F. Cloud secure connection

An issue when cloud purchaser use applications and information depends on relationship from different fogs; it needs to keep up its security rudiments attested on the two fogs and in within. This issue can be fixed by character connection, using character properties affiliation, single sign-on, check, and endorsing can help settle organization security issues.

G. Different Stakeholders

- ✓ Different adornments in coursed figuring are
- ✓ Cloud provider, one who passes on the establishment to cloud customers.
- ✓ The ace center, one who uses cloud establishment to pass on applications for end customers.

Customer, one who uses the affiliation bolstered in a cloud zone.

Most of the above has their security issues. Each customer will have explicit trust relationship of providers; every once in a while customer himself can be struck. Provider and customer need to agree on conditions.

H. Pariah Control

The owner has no impact over their data getting ready as this is a distant issue. Cloud providers don't think about the structure of Cloud, so fantastic security isn't given. Now and then the customer can be dashed with one vender. This occurs because of a perception or trouble in moving the data to the new shipper.

I. Uprightness of information

The uprightness of information is created when there is a run of the mill trust in the provider and purchaser, and they supplement each other and support the security to such a degree, that the structure works constantly. To achieve this genuine insistence, guaranteeing and accounting controls should be executed by the cloud pro association and customer. The capacities to get agree to the information on the cloud should be individualized, secure (RSA tokens or one-time perplex express) and should not be shared among the substances of the purchaser association.

II J. Denial of information

The buyer and the provider ended up in a tremendous hole concerning appearing completed was by them or not. To evade this issue at cloud level, cloud provider needs to ensure that non-denial engaged show or handshake is sent whereby, pulling in social gatherings can't dismiss their help with the battle trade.

K. Affiliation impediments

It can arrive any business/relationship in a chafing condition, the information required isn't available when it is most required and unpalatable lead can be recognized by DOS, DDOS trap. This issue can be tended to by using the cutoff all around way to deal with have security controls recognized at various layers all through the cloud get to path equivalently as inside the purchaser and provider engineer, sharing of record capacities between purchasers should be deliberately denied.

L. Loss of Control

Loss of control can be a debacle for an association. This is one of the CIO's genuine stresses before they move their data/information to the cloud. To constrain this effects, the affiliations should esteem the cloud provider's security structures, amassing frameworks, and SLAs. This will engage in shared insight between the provider and client about the way by which the purchaser data will be directed in the cloud.

Checked Cloud Architecture

Security remains to be a stress for customers as they set out to move to the cloud. In any case, a couple of bits of an ensured establishment are fundamental to various customer affiliations. To satisfy security necessities and address the security issues are hardened as examined above, various security issues by the cloud security structure.

A. Single Sign-On

Everything considered, the client of the cloud will have moving logins, regardless of this will prompt check issues, so solid declaration at client level ought to be given inside the cloud.

B. Increase Availability

To expand the information comfort dynamic server loads altering and ISP weight changing inside the structure framework.

C. Check in Depth Approach

There should be reasonable interruption recognizing evidence and avoiding parts inside the system. The Proper virtual firewall ought to be executed instead of extraordinary firewalls. Interruption adjusting movement structures (IPS) ought to be familiar with shield systems from inside dangers from insiders.

D. Single Management Console

Additional system security gadgets ought to be utilized to ensure virtual structure this single connection solace ought to be utilized.

The central focuses could be a dash of the doable for the all inclusive community that offer circled enrolling based affiliations and applications.

Cost Savings

Affiliations could lessen their capital uses and utilize operational uses by expanding their taking care of cutoff points. This would be a lower farthest point to area and requires less in-house IT framework preferences for offer help.

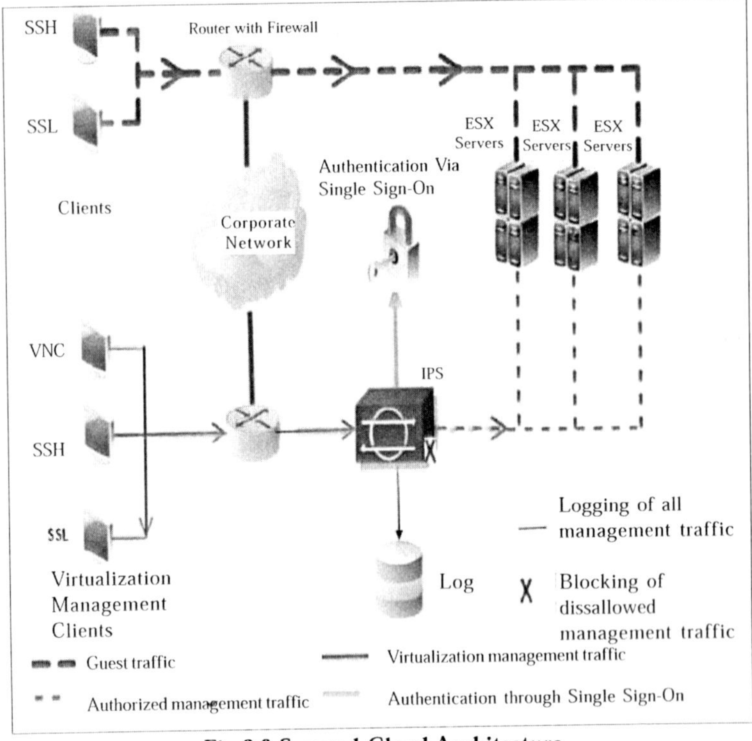

Fig 3.6 Secured Cloud Architecture

Advantages and Challenges

Scalability/Flexibility

Affiliations could begin with a little strategy and build up a colossal sending quickly, and after that scale back at whatever point required. In like way, the versatility of circled preparing would empower endeavors to utilize an additional asset at peak times, drawing in them to satisfy client requests.

Reliability

Associations would utilize particular dull objectives could bolster business comprehension and disaster recuperation.

Maintenance

Cloud ace networks could give the structure upkeep and could access through APIs that would not require application strategy into PCs, all things considered further reducing protection necessities.

Mobile Accessibility

Smaller specialists may have broadened productivity because of frameworks open to a foundation accessible from anywhere.Some of the conspicuous difficulties would be associated with passed on enrolling, but then a touch of these inconveniences may cause a log jam when giving more associations in the cloud, and gives openings. On the off chance that an issue exists, suppliers could offer associations to mind and show thought in the planning stages.

Security and Privacy

Conceivably two of the more "hot catch" could be an issue consolidating passed on handling identify with verifying and affirming information and review the use of the cloud by the ace focuses. These issues could be regularly credited to diminishing approach of cloud associations. These inconveniences could be tended to, by verifying the data inside the alliance nevertheless empowering it to be utilized in the cloud. For this to occur, regardless, the security instruments between the alliance and the cloud required to be excited and a Hybrid Cloud could strengthen such a course of action.

Lack of Standards

Hazes could have seen interfaces; regardless, no models would be associated with these, and therefore it could be unimaginable that most mists would be interoperable. The Open Grid Forum could be stirring up an Open Cloud Computing Interface to choose this issue, and the Open Cloud Consortium would handle appropriated figuring standards and practices. The disclosures of these get-togethers would need to develop, yet it isn't known whether they will address the necessities of the general open passing on the associations and the particular interfaces to these association prerequisites. Regardless, keeping alert with the latest on the most recent standards as they would empower them to be utilized, if legitimate

Continuously Evolving

Client deals would be constantly made, as the necessities for interfaces, structures association, and cutoff. This proposes a "cloud," particularly an open one, would not be static but rather unendingly makes.

Compliance Concerns

The Sarbanes-Oxley Act (SOX) in the US and Data Protection directions in the EU (European) are having different consistence issues affecting dispersed figuring. They will propose what cloud could utilize subject to the portrayal of information and application. The EU has a legitimate sponsorship of information assurance for all part states, yet in the US information affirmation would be exceptional and could move from state to state. In like way with security and protection imparted starting at now, these usually results from Hybrid cloud sending of one cloud verifying the information inner to the connection.

4

MAP REDUCE TECHNIQUE AS A PROGRAMMING MODEL FOR PROCESSING IN CLOUD COMPUTING

4.1 INTRODUCTION

The present cloud system and the related affiliations can capably and pleasingly reinforce little applications with moderate resource nuts and bolts. Regardless, fogs accomplish their hindrances when overseeing Big Data applications that require a titanic number of ideal conditions, fast scaling or regular preparing. A particular multifaceted and disturbing piece of the data the administrators for Big Data applications is overseeing data transversely over wide territories over the geologically circled cloud server ranches. Nowadays, a creating number of managing conditions and applications require such dealing with.

4.1.1 Map reduction Frame Work

Guide Reduce is a programming model for managing huge informational social affairs with a parallel, floated computation on a pack. A Map Reduce program is made out of a Map() structure that performs isolating and orchestrating, for instance, dealing with understudies by first name into lines, one line for each name and a Reduce() methodology that plays out a summation task, for instance, including the proportion of understudies in each line, yielding name frequencies. The Map Reduce System empowers by marshaling the disseminated servers, running the various errands in parallel, managing all trades and data moves between the various bits of the structure, obliging overabundance and change as per inward disappointment, and standard talking relationship of the whole methodology.

The model is blended by the guide and lessens works normally used in utilitarian programming, disregarding the way where that their inspiration in the Map Reduce framework isn't equal to their emerge structures. Furthermore, the key commitment of the Map Reduce framework are not the authentic guide and lessening cutoff focuses, regardless the versatility and change as per trivial disappointment achieved for an arrangement of employments by improving the execution engine once. Guide Reduce libraries have been written in many programming vernaculars, with different degrees of advancement. A common open source use is Apache Hadoop.

The name Map Reduce at first recommended the world class Google progress and has since been aggregate up. Guide Reduce is a structure for managing parallelizable issues across over tremendous datasets using endless PCs (centers), everything considered inferred as a pack if each center point are on a comparable abutting framework and use proportionate contraption or a system if within centers are shared transversely over topographically and truly coursed systems and use progressively heterogeneous hardware. Computational managing can occur on educational accumulation away either in a record structure (unstructured) or in a database (managed). Guide Reduce can misuse zone of data, managing data on or close quite far tendencies for decreasing transmission of data. An authority center may do this again thusly, influencing a bewildered tree structure. The authority center point shapes the more diminutive issue and passes the sensible reaction back to its ruler center.

Decrease step: The star center point by then gathers the reactions to all the sub-issues and associations them by one way or another or another to design the yield – the reaction to the issue was at first attempting to understand. Guide Reduce considers scattered treatment of the guide and rot works out. Given each mapping undertaking is free of the others, all maps can be performed in parallel regardless at last it is compelled by the proportion of autonomous data sources correspondingly as the proportion of CPUs near each source. Moreover, a great deal of 'reducers' can play out the lessening organize - if all yields of the guide movement that offer a comparative key are appeared to a relative reducer meanwhile, or if beyond what many would consider possible is characteristic. While this strategy can an extraordinary piece of the time have every one of the reserves of being inefficient meandered from figurings that are intelligently powerful

Guide Reduce can be connected with all around more conspicuous datasets than thing servers can administer. A monster server can use Map Reduce to sort a petabyte (thousand terabytes) of data in only a couple of hours. The parallelism in like manner offers some believability of recovering from midway disappointment of servers or limit during the undertaking. In case one mapper or reducer crashes and burns, the work can be rescheduled – persevering through the data is so far open.

Another way to deal with oversee see Map Reduce is as a 5-step parallel and dispersed count.

1. Prepare the Map() input – the "Guide Reduce structure" doles out Map processors, names the K1 data key worth each processor would wear out, and gives that processor all of the data related with that key worth.

2. Run the customer gave Map () code – Map () is run certainly once for each K1 key worth, making yield overseen by key characteristics K2.

3. "Shuffle" the Map respect the Reduce processors – the Map Reduce structure dispatches Reduce processors, doles out the K2 key worth each processor would regulate and

outfits that processor with all the Map-made data related with that key worth.

4. Run the customer gave Reduce() code – Reduce() is run surely once for each K2 key worth passed on by the Map step

5. Produce the last yield – the Map Reduce structure hoards all the Reduce yield, and sorts it by K2 to pass on a definitive outcome. Very these 5 phases can be thought of as running in plan – every advancement starts fundamentally after the past progress is done – regardless at last, undeniably, they can be entwined, as long as the last result isn't influenced

Genuinely these 5 phases can be thought of as running in development – every improvement starts fundamentally after the past headway is done regardless all around that truly matters, clearly, they can be joined, as long as the last result isn't influenced Map Reduce is an ability to package out work to various concentrations inside get-together and organize and rot the result from each center point into a firm reaction to request. Its pieces: I) PAAS tracker 2) work tracer3) work history server

Guide Reduce framework, it is for getting ready and making beast datasets with parallel, appropriated rely upon a get-together. It is obviously not hard to use for undertakings without fuse with parallel and distributive structure since it covers the nuances of parallelization, acclimation to non-crucial dissatisfaction and region improvement. According to Pankaj Singh et al (2014), Ankur et al(2014),chandhany et al(2014) immense degree of issues are sufficient expressible as Map Reduce check .Map-step handle a little issue Hoop's pack segment the issue into little subset and pick those to control system to get it. Decrease diminishes the conceivable consequence of mapping strategy and structures the yield of the Map Reduce movement

4.2 DATA PROCESSING MODELS: MAPREDUCE ON CLOUDS

Data managing is another significant perspective that ought to be considered concerning Big Data, as understanding its characteristics structures the best methodologies. Regardless, with the progression of the figure conditions, particular managing systems are, ported on the cloud or on huge establishments, in order to address the application bothers. The most remarkable of them is the Map Reduce managing. Close-by with structures that execute this perspective. The rule weight to use the coding approach of Hadoop Map Reduce is that hadoop bosses need to make a couple of lines out of focal java code requiring extra effort and time for code consider. As necessities be, to loosen up this Apache offers various decisions like Pig Latin and Hive SQL dialects that help in structure Map Reduce programs tastefully. Regardless, the bit of room is that Map Reduce gives more control to forming complex business premise when showed up contrastingly in association with Pig and Hive.

4.2.1 Data Generalization with Map Reduce

In monstrous information applications, information security is a legend among the most concerned issues since preparing colossal scale attestation sensitive illuminating records now and again requires figuring power given by open cloud affiliations. Sub-tree information Anonymization, getting a regular exchange off between information utility and bending, is a perceptibly comprehended course of action to anonymize educational records for confirmation guaranteeing. Top-Down Specialization (TDS) and Bottom-Up Generalization (BUG) are two excellent ways to deal with oversee satisfy sub-tree Anonymization. Regardless, existing frameworks for Sub-tree Anonymization miss the mark with deference beyond what many would consider possible, in that limit missing adaptability in regulating monster information on cloud Still, both TDS and BUG experience discouraging having all the earmarks of being certain estimation of k-absence of lucidity parameter in the event that they are used straightforwardly. In this paper, a cream method is shown which joins TDS and BUG for feasible sub-tree Anonymization over huge information. Further, plan Map Reduce based strategies two bits (TDS and BUG) to extend high adaptability by manhandling shocking tally most extreme of cloud. The crossbreed approach on a chief level improves the adaptability and farthest point of sub-tree Anonymization plot over existing structures.

The fundamental illuminating get-together is summed up for information Anonymization by a one-pass Map Reduce work. Past what many would consider conceivable passes on darken records and its check as appeared by the present Anonymization level. The Reduce wear down an incredibly central level techniques these dull records and checks their number. An abnormal record and its check address a QI-gathering, and the QI-wraps set up the last dull edifying reports.

Speculation: In this method, single estimations of properties are dislodged by with a perseveringly wide course of action. For instance, the worth '19' of the property 'Age' might be supplanted by ' = 20', the worth '23' by '20 < Age = 30'.

Base Up Generalization (BUG) is one of the beneficial k-Anonymization approaches. K-Anonymity where the characteristics are covered up or summed until each locale is dull with in any event k-1 unquestionable lines. A little while later database is said to be k concealed. Base Up Generalization (BUG) approach of Anonymization is the course toward beginning from the least Anonymization level which is iteratively performed. The effect affirmation exchange off as the intrigue metric Bottom-Up Generalization and MR (Map Reduce) Bottom up Generalization (MRBUG) Driver are utilized. The going with undertakings of the Advanced BUG are, they are information portion, run MRBUG Driver on illuminating record, join all Anonymization levels of the apportioned information things and after that apply speculation to novel illuminating social affair without culpable the k-inconclusive quality Figure 3.2. Structure plan of base up techniques here an astoundingly made Bottom-Up Generalization approach which improves the versatility and execution of BUG. Two degrees of parallelization which is finished by guide diminish (MR) on cloud condition. Guide lessen on cloud has two degrees of parallelization. First is work level parallelization which means obvious MR occupations can be executed while uses cloud framework. Second one is errand level parallelization which comprehends that distinctive mapper or reducer assignments in a MR Job are executed meanwhile on information scatterings. The going with advances are performed in our way of thinking,

The k-nonappearance of lucidity structure has been used to clarify the security in passed on figuring condition. The k-reasons packaging framework has likewise been utilized for at first assembling the layout of records given as information. The k-secret principal and the data occasion are checked for every get-together to change the pack formed by the k-deduces gathering approach. The new record included is then checked with each get-together and it is united with a pack subject to the k-namelessness prevention. The grown-up dataset has been utilized for our experimentation and confined the reinforced system and a current Xuyun Zhang et al's. structure dependent on the time taken to restore for the new records.

This recommendation got a few information about the versatility issue of sub-tree anonymization over Big-Data and proposed Descend Traversal Prioritization (DTP) and Ascend Traversal Abstraction (ATA) as it gives favored feasibility over the present structures, for example, Top – Down Specialization (TDS) and Bottom – Up Generalization (BUG). To be always versatile to the degree limit both DTP and ATA are joined to shape another HYBRID viewpoint for sub-tree data anonymization detached and existing frameworks Map Reduce, Dean et al (2010), Ghenawat et al (2010) a huge scale data masterminding structure, have been asked with cloud to give check most far off point concerning applications, for example Amazon Elastic Map Reduce (EMR) association. It impacts Map Reduce to address the adaptability issue in our framework. As the Map Reduce arranging is the perfect model for Big-Data Anonymization utilizing the DTP and ATA approaches.

4.3 ANONYMIZATION METHODOLOGY

Current structures for security ensuring will be discovered wasteful in the going with couple of years when new refined ambushes make. There are four sorts of request securing approach reliably utilized for managing the issue of the de-unquestionable attestation structure: K-Anonymity, L-Diversity, T-Closeness and Differential Privacy. These structures still have vulnerabilities. The standard issues of these framework are fragile information presentation (K-Anonymity), semantic similarity of unsure information (L-Diversity), separate measures (T-Closeness), and the control of the fuel level added to the business yield Differential Privacy.

4.3.1 Sub – Tree Generalization

Our examination, thusly, pivots the sub-tree speculation plan. Not in the scarcest degree like multidimensional or cell hypothesis plans, sub-tree theory can explain obscure data that may be obviously used by existing data mining. This technique offers an ordinary trade off between data utility and data consistency. In this way, this technique has been all around broke down.

Top–down specialization [TDS] and base up hypothesis [BUG] are two classes of timetables to fulfill the sub-tree theory plan. Most leaving checks try referencing data structure to help the strategy for Anonymization. Especially, TIPS (Taxonomy Indexed Partitions) for top–down specialization and TEA (Taxonomy Encoded Anonymity) record for base up theory. Such a lot of referencing data structures can restore the system of data Anonymization, these systems more often than not rejection to work in parallel or passed on conditions like cloud structures in light of the way that the referencing structures are joined. Mohammed et al (2010) proposed a passed on top–down specialization approach which, not withstanding, on a basic level concerns assertion affirmation from various surfaces rather than adaptability issues. Everything considered, this framework just uses information gets as the referencing metric, coming about lower data utility than joined ones. The past work Zhang et al (2014) impacts Map Reduce.

Tremendous Data Anonymization for example giant data anonymization is cleaned through top–down specialization. Meanwhile top–down specialization in actuality performs slower than base up theory when k-confound parameter k is associated with nothing.

Adaptability and attainability of Anonymization estimations for security guaranteeing has drawn thought of reviewers. R-tree referencing, adaptable choice trees and testing frameworks consider achieve high adaptability and breaking point, Lefevre et al (2008), Iwuchukwu et al(2007). In any case, the proposed techniques go for multidimensional theory plan, thusly expulsion to work for sub-tree speculation.

4.3.2 Map Reduce Framework

Anonymization improvement is major for accomplishing affirmation on security when utilizing single information. In the time of goliath information a huge amount of data has been totaled on the planet. There are issues where in individual are Identified by planning with other information. Anonymization in monster information is a test to change over important information into non explicit information. With the assistance of the guide decreasing structure the tremendous number of affiliations and relationship to process colossal volume illuminating records. Affirmation checking and high utility of Data is conceivable in light of the guide decreasing structure.

Guide Reduce has been routinely gotten in various data managing uses to support flexibility and ampleness K.Lefevre et al (2008), Enene et al (2011), Palit et al (2012), Vernica et al (2010), on titanic data Anonymization.

Guide Reduce is a programming model for overseeing and passing on huge instructive records with a parallel, spread rely upon a party. Limit relative points of view have been especially imperative with the message passing interface standard having abatement and scatter works out. A Map spoil program is made out of a Map () framework that performs disengaging and arranging and a diminishing structure that plays out a system works out. The "Guide Reduce System" designs the overseeing by marshaling the dissipated servers, running the different assignments in parallel, dealing with all exchanges and information moves between the different bits of the structure and obliging emphasis and change according to inside disappointment.

Hadoop surrounded on java that licenses to store and process tremendous data in scattered condition transversely over party of PCs using key programming model. It was displayed in 2004. Hadoop is an Apache open source structure. It's verifiably not a sort of database it is a thing eco structure that contemplates gigantically parallel choosing which attract of certain NOSQL dispersed database which can draw in data to be spread across over unlimited servers with little diminishing in execution. A stable Hadoop regular framework is Map Reduce computational model and spread the estimation over a conceivably relentless number of servers. Data can be inspected with the help of Hadoop. HDFS Hadoop can work clearly with any mountable circled record system, yet most essential report structure used by HDFS .It relies on Google archive structure (GFS) .The advantages of HDFS is that it allows quickly passed on system and does not rely on contraption change as per inside disappointment and exceedingly openness. Affiliations can be joined or ousted cleverly without interruption and it is impeccable on most of the phases since it is java based. The piece of HDFS is fitting for encompassed totaling and masterminding. It outfits request interface with HDFT .The server of the name center and server homestead direct serves toward adequately check the status of the gathering and gives record underwriting and affirmation.

Guide Reduce is a thing structure for successfully encircling applications which method huge degrees of data (multi-terabyte illuminating records) in-parallel on massive packs (a critical number of center centers) of thing gear in a trustworthy, defect tolerant way.

A Map Reduce work overall parts the data enlightening social event into free inconsistencies which are set up by the guide attempts in a totally parallel manner. The structure sorts the yields of the maps, which are then guarantee to the decreasing errands. Commonly both the information and the yield of the advancement are confirmed in a record structure. The framework directs booking has a go at, watching them and re-executes the shelled errands.

Dependably the technique center concentrations and the limit centers are the identical, that is, the Map Reduce structure and the Hadoop Distributed File System are running on a close diagram of core interests. This course of action empowers the structure to conceivably design assignments within centers where data is starting at now present, recognizing unbelievably high full scale information transmission over the get-together.

The Map Reduce structure incorporates single ace Job Tracker and one slave Task Tracker for each pack center point. The mater is Responsible for engineering the occupations' part takes a stab at the slaves, checking them and re-executing the assaulted assignments. The slaves execute the endeavors as made by the master.

4.4 DESCEND TRAVERSAL PRIORITIZATION (DTP) AND ASCEND TRAVERSAL ABSTRACTION (ATA) USING MAPREDUCE

The Descend Traversal Prioritization and Ascend Traversal Abstraction using Map Reduce are told as a touch of this district. Fundamentally, a Map Reduce undertaking unites Map and Reduce works close to a Driver that controls the Map Reduce occupations. The explained explanation may be seen in. To refresh the adaptability and sufficiency of our procedure, parallelization degree is upheld, Uyun et al (2014), Hang et al (2014).

4.4.1 Map Reduce Driver

On an exceptionally fundamental level, both Descend Traversal Prioritization (DTP) and Ascend Traversal Abstraction (ATA) methods of Anonymization are an iterative system starting from the most amazing and least Anonymization levels openly. Fall Traversal Prioritization is the specialization through dealing with the class portions with the client indicated k – namelessness parameter anyway Ascend Traversal Abstraction is the speculation through portraying the sub trees as key terms. Rather than taking relationship of more sub trees, theoretical is seen as where novel is the social event of sub trees. The least Anonymization level contains the inward space center concentrations in the most decreased degree of coherent course of action trees while the higher Anonymization level contains a tantamount that of the concentrations in more prominent total. Each round of accentuation joins.

Documentations utilized in figuring:

- D-An educational social affair containing records
- D*-Anonymized dataset
- AGSET-open speculation set
- SGSET-family speculation set
- NGSET-new speculation set
- AL-Anonymization level
- K-absence of definition parameter

Four genuine advances:

1. Checking the present informational get-together whether satisfies the absence of clearness level, finding the ILPG, finding the best prioritization and summing up the illuminating document as appeared by the picked best prioritization.
2. Figuring the ILPG (Information Loss per security gain)
3. Summing up the enlightening social event circuit getting to a wide number of data records, as such overpowering the flexibility and feasibility of both Descend Traversal Prioritization and Ascend Traversal Abstraction.
4. The current system Ke et al(2004) utilizes prioritization and impression of mentioning data structure and holding truth information to overhaul the effectiveness. In any case the methodology encounters poor flexibility and capacity

in enormous data circumstance. In any case, the technique fails to be balanced into Map Reduce since Map Reduce does not abstain from mentioning data structure.

4.4.2 Novel Map Reduce

Everything thought of it as, proposes to make novel Map lessen associations for the ILPG figuring. As idea of Anonymization level thinks about portray Anonymization status of illuminating social affair, it is superfluous to aggregate up the educational rundown solidly in each round as to effectiveness. Or then again potentially, proficiently total up the instructive list over the present Anonymization level. After the last Anonymization level is gotten, anonymize the illuminating get-together in a one-pass Map decrease work.

4.4.3 Algorithm: Map Reduce (MR) Ascend traversal abstraction

Input: Data set D, Anonymization level AL_n, anonymity parameter k.

Output: Initial anonymous data set D*

1) Initialize the values of search metric ILPG for each prioritization with respect to AL ,via job ILPG Calculation;
2) Sort out and generate the possible prioritization (pri).
3) While pri, A_c(pri)>k
4) Identify the available prioritization set AG Set out of all the active prioritization candidates;
5) Vpri AGset, label gen as INACTIVE to perform gen on the current anonymization level;
6) pri AGset, Vpri' SGset (gen), gen' is already labeled as INACTIVE;
7) Insert a new prioritization pri_{New}:Child(q) ->q into NGSet, where Child(qi)={q|pri :Child(q)q, pri¸ GSet(pri)}remove all prioritizations in SGSet(pri);end ifAL_I<- AL_{I+1}; Update

ILPG values for all active prioritization candidates in AL_l via $_l$LPG Calculation; end while Prioritize D to D in terms of ALi, via job Data Prioritization.

4.4.4 Algorithm 2: Map Reduce (MR) Descend traversal prioritization

Calculation 1 and 2 portrays the Map Reduce Driver for Descend Traversal Prioritization and Ascend Traversal Abstraction. It requires ILPG accepting that unites getting to the central educational list and arranging point of convergence information over the enlightening file and also needs managing the whole instructive accumulation To update Map Reduce to lead the genuine reprisal in these conditions. Especially, diagram a few novel Map Reduce occupations: the work ILPG figuring for accomplishing the calculation required, and the development information prioritization for achieving the last strong Anonymization. In the going with a region, dismember how to help the parallelization of performing speculation in each round of cycle, for the sole reason behind improving versatility and ability of DTP and ATA.

4.4.5 Parallelization of Performing Generalizations

A few recognitions obviously help to plot able Map Reduce occupations for the ILPG Calculation. One is that, not at all like Descend Traversal Prioritization that inserts a few new need candidates into the present anonymization level in each round; Ascend Traversal Abstraction just implants another special contender after a couple of rounds of considering. An other is that driving a counsel won't influence the information loss of an other reflection sure to the degree Wang et al (2012). Taking such affirmations, consider diverse reflection contenders into record in one round, along these lines improving the degree of parallelization and the sufficiency of the strategy. Notwithstanding, playing out a counsel maybe changes the riddle of the instructive social occasion and security increase of each reflection contender will be influenced.

4.4.6 ILPG calculation job

The ILPG Calculation job is capable to initialize ILPG. The processing needed in ILPG instatement is very like that of ILPG redesign. The Map capacity of the ILPG Calculation, while the Reduce functions is exhibited.

Algorithm 3: ILPG calculation map

Input: Data record (IDr, r),r D; Anonymization level AL, NGSet.

Output: Intermediate key-value pair (key, count).

1) For each attribute value v_i in r, find its generalization in current AL: gen_i. Let p_i be the parent in gen_i, and c_i be v_i itself or p_i' child that is also V_i' ancestor;

2) If $gen_i \in$ NGset, emit (($p_{i,}$ $c_{i,}$ SV), count);

3) Construct quasi-identifier qid = (q_1, q_2, . . ., q_m), where

$$q_i = \begin{cases} p_i & \text{if } gen_i \text{ is } INACTIVE \\ C_i & o.w., \end{cases} \quad 1 \le i \le m; Emit\,((qid, \$\#), count);$$

4) For each I [1,m], replace q_i in qid with its parent p_i ifq_i =c_i, producing the resultant quasi-identifier

For ILPG introduction, NGSet is the collection of all the introductory generalizations concerning AL_0, while for ILPG redesigns and changes a unique record into its anonymized structure as indicated by the current anonymization level, for the sole purpose of being numbered. Data misfortune is figured, discharges the key-worth pair to the Reduce capacity for data misfortune calculation if this pair is another generalization applicant. Note that the data loss of a generalization won't be influenced when we perform different generalizations or supplement another generalization, while protection increase will most likely be affected as the secrecy of the data set will change.

Algorithm 4: ILPG calculation reduce

Input: Intermediate key-value pair (key, list (count)).

Output: Information gain (gen, IL (gen)) and anonymity (gen, (Ac(gen), AQISet)),(gen, A_p(gen))for prioritization.

1) For each key, sumCount;
2) For each key, if key.sv #, update statistical counts:
3) If all sensitive values for child c have arrived, computeI(R_c);
4) If all children c of parent p have arrived, compute I (R_p) and IL(gen);emit(gen, IL(gen));
5) For each key, if key.sv=#, update anonymity:
6) If key. c =$ and sum<A_p(gen), update current anonymity :A_p (gen)<- sum;
7) If key '" $:
8) If sum<A_c(gen),update potential anonymity of gen:A_c(gen)<- sum and AQI Set<- key.
9) If sum=A_c(gen), update :AQI Set<- {key. c} AQI Set;
10) Emit (gen, A_p (gen)) and emit (gen,(A_c(gen), AQISet)).

The Reduce work primarily totals the factual data to ascertain data misfortune and protection pick up. The main part, computes data loss in terms. Because of that the key-worth sets are sorted by Map Reduce inherent component before being sustained to Reducer specialists, the Reduce capacity can figure data loss for generalizations in grouping, without obliging extensive measure of memory to holding measurable data. Along these lines, the Reduce capacity is very versatile for computing data loss, Xuyun Hang et al (2014)

The crucial of figuring secrecy of an information set is to figure out the base QI-group size. The second part goes for computing protection gain and distinguishing AQI Set. The Reducer laborers figure out the generally least QI-group size previously, then after performing a generalization in parallel. At that point, get the internationally one in the driver program through contrasting the yields of Reducer specialists. The quasi-identifiers of the QI-bunches with the base gathering size are recorded amid the methodology and constitute AQI Set. Note that AQI Set assumes a paramount part in recognizing accessible generalizations in the following round of emphasis. Most importantly, the ILPG Calculation Reduce capacity is very versatile for both data loss and security gain calculation. In the wake of acquiring data misfortune and security pick up, ascertain ILPG values.

4.4.7 Data Generalization

The essential educational social affair is truly theory for data Anonymization by a one-pass Map Reduce work, i.e., Data Generalization. Nuances of Map and Reduce portions of the data specialization Map Reduce occupation can be explained in . Xuyun Z.Hang et al(2014). Beyond what many would consider possible transmits shrouded records and its check as appeared by the present Anonymization level. The Reduce work in a general sense demonstrates these astounding records and checks their number. A dazing record and its check address a QI-gathering, and the QI-packs incorporate the last dim enlightening accumulations.

4.5 HYBRID APPROACH FOR SUB-TREE ANONYMIZATION

In this part, in a general sense dismantle how to join the Descend Traversal Prioritization and Ascend Traversal Abstraction together in the proposed mutt framework. The cream perspective which picks fragments therefore by disconnecting the k-question key with a framework parameter is outlined out quickly further. By at that point, reveal how to quantify the parameter and change the parameter as showed up by the information skewness to invigorate the execution of our system.

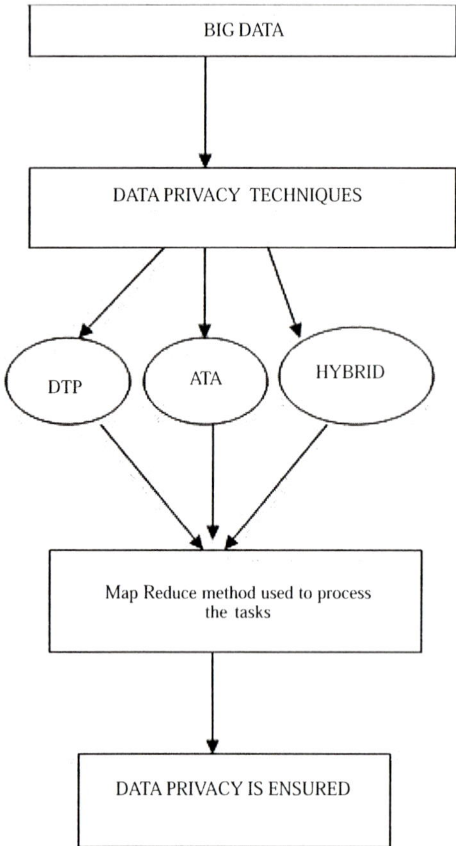

Figure 4.1 Overall System Architecture

4.5.1 Combining Descend Traversal Prioritization and Ascend Traversal Abstraction

Presently the Map Reduce form of Ascend Traversal Abstraction (MRATA) and Descend Traversal Prioritization (MRDTP) have been created in the last area, the two segments, i.e., MRDTP and MRATA, are prepared for the proposed hybrid methodology of sub-tree Anonymization over huge information. As far as the issue dissection, to figure out which segment is utilized to anonymize information after the secrecy parameter k is detailed by a client. It is guaranteeing that the hybrid approach can consequently give out a framework parameter K such that if k, MRDTP is chosen, overall MRATA is chosen. Formally, characterize this limit as Workload Balancing Point.

Input: Data set D; k-anonymity parameter k.

Output: Anonymous dataset.

B. If k k, anonymize D with MRDTP;

C. else, anonymize D with MRATA.

Algorithm 5: Hybrid approach

Evaluating the careful estimation of K is difficult since K vigorously relies upon a few properties of information sets, in the same way as information appropriation and skewness. On the other hand, it is unnecessary to get the definite quality in light of the fact that the execution of MRDTP and MRATA simply has a little effect when k is esteemed around K. Accordingly, to assess the quality k as per the extent of the information set and scientific classification trees in the accompanying segment.

4.5.2Skewness -Aware Workload Balancing Point Adjustment (WBPA)

Note that informative records are truly scattered in the last region when assessing the amazing weight changing point K. In most certifiable informative gatherings, in any case, the information disseminating is routinely not utilizing all strategies yet incline, which impacts the concerning of K. Slip Traversal Prioritization and Ascend Traversal Abstraction are single dimensional Sparkling framework for sub-tree anonymization plan B.C.M Fung et al (2010). As appeared by a theory in K. Lefevre et al.(2006), the most amazing QI-bunch size of an unacknowledged illuminating social event D occurring in light of either DTP or ATA is O (|D |). To staggering degree incline instructive social occasion can influence tremendous QI-pack measure. On the off chance that such an edifying collection is anonymized by systems for DTP, two or three specializations can accomplish the objective. Ordinarily, the more inclination an instructive rundown is, the area MRDTP is coherently kept up in the cream approach, in light of the way in which that practicing inclination edifying record will play out the last k-baffle enlightening amassing significantly speedier than summing up low level zone regards in MRATA. Along these lines, it is basic and sensible to modify K as appeared by the skewness of information spreading.

To effect change of the information strategy to alter the estimation of extra major occupation modifying point (K). The ability can get the dissipating of the scattering of semi identifier properties. On the off chance that what has any sort of impact is zero, the information courses of all attributes will be uniform. For this condition, K does not require change. On the off chance that the change is colossal, it prescribes that the scatterings of trademark attributes are odd as opposed to undertaking and, i.e., some zone qualities take liberally a more essential number of information records than others.

This case can actuate keen infringement of the k-mystery need when performing Descend Traversal Prioritization. Beginning now and into the not so distant, high refinement lean towards MRDTP, and should reducing the estimation of K to make the shot of picking MRATA. In like way, higher change means lower K with the target that MRDTP is effectively bolstered in relationship with higher capacity. Particularly, utilize a parameter to change K, this parameter is known to be adjustment.

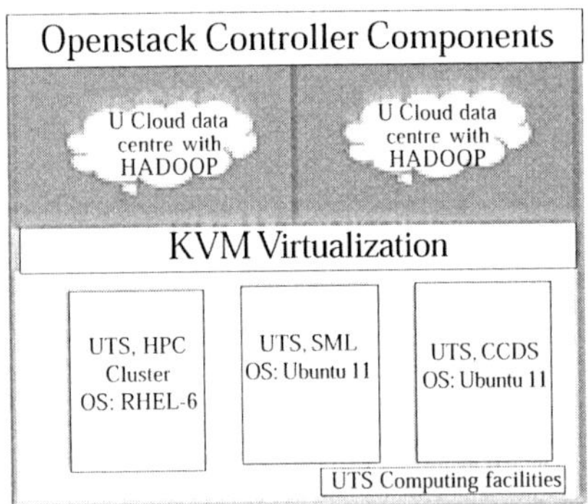

Figure 4.2 System Overview of U-Cloud

Cv_{max} is the most extreme worth among C_{vi} , $1 < i < m$, i.e., Cv_{max} = max1 <i< m Cv_i . Since Cv_i might be esteemed more noteworthy than 1, we further standardize them so as to bind their qualities in . At that point, the mean of the coefficients of variety of all disseminations likewise extends in. As far as the previously stated instinct that decreases while the scattering of the information circulations develops, It characterize the estimation of to be 1 less the mean of coefficients of variance. At the point when the difference is 0 (coefficient of variance will be 0 likewise), is esteemed 1 and no change is obliged, which is the perfect situation where conveyances are even as examined. To ascertain, we have to determine Mij from the information set. A basic however Map Reduce work that emits each attribute value and count their occurrence.

In More skewness, MRDTP is more favored in hybrid; modifying K should be done as per the skewness of information. When the difference between skewness and MRDTP is zero, all quality will be uniform, here balance is not necessary.

5

CONCLUSION AND FUTURE WORK

In present time, cloud based improvements have made as a computational model that might be used to meet out the continually expanding overseeing and cutoff necessities of current applications. The fundamental purpose of combination of this examination is inducing information get to, improved structure, better mechanical social occasions and beneficial conglomerating in appropriated choosing. The contraptions like Aneka, Hadoop, NoSQL and Flink are investigated during examination work for making skilled and checked information access models, streamlined weight changing of favorable circumstances for meet the client fundamentals and looking procedures by frameworks for their upsides and disadvantages.

5.1 CONCLUSION

There are two or three different models of passed on figuring. There exists much open structure, multi source data structure, security influenced orchestrating accessible recorded as a printed copy, yet for no circumstance one of them can give hard and fast reaction for refinement of sales terms which are constrained from Internet. Consequently, its answer lies in the likelihood of thoughtful perspective, which hopes to make affiliations and relationship among these ousted reports with the target that client may tastefully watch such records and use their relationship through customers. The cloud suppliers offer such relationship as pay per use. This proposed cloud data organizing reasonably manages the pensive perspective age for standard diagram of cloud assets and messages which are affirmed on cloud customers.

It ends up less heavenly for client to get to information and affiliations utilizing demand recovery structure in the wake of get-together information at one spot. This instrument channels and refines them as proper or futile. The proposed model in like way gives arrangement of reusing produces results for at some point, rather than the Grep plan. What's more it other than makes search reliably refined.

Cloud security is one of key concerns which similarly should be tended to. Regardless, circled dealing with gives flexible and straightforwardness to utilize benefits in any case on the off chance that information isn't kept secure, by then it is of no use. Cloud benchmarks must be kept in the frame of mind for guaranteeing realness and puzzler.

With the assistance of virtualization, it has been demonstrated that the method for information from cloud by utilizing systems like Para-virtualization, memory virtualization, gear virtualization, and so on has been made much continuously clear and momentous. It has attempted in this recommendation our proposed model for getting to Desktop as a Service utilizing memory virtualization approach in cloud condition is determinedly astonishing and supportive. This framework introductions to have higher information capacity with less level of infringement of SLAs. It is likewise seen here that the shadow paging recuperation framework utilized in the cloud structures spares assets if there should be an occasion of framework bafflement. It has been likely demonstrated that the proposed string sorting out figuring Mat Matcher that yields for a specific model entered by the client in the cloud is talented and astounding. The proposed structure can deal with the two numbers in like manner as letters all together and appropriately utilizes the sensible framework to introduce the properties that show the closeness and nonattendance of model in the substance. The proposed figuring is well test and examined for better execution against existing standard string organizing structures.

An improved planning check to reduce superb weight and to change occupations errand concerning task in Hadoop stage is dissected. The proposed affirmation control and the heuristic based way to deal with oversee direct improve the heap changing and work throughput and to diminish the standard bomb rate of occupation is tended to.

The information stores like NoSQL, NewSQL have offered themselves as decisions instead of standard social databases, planned administering epic volumes of information on passed on choosing condition. Basically more sensibly, this suggestion has audited NoSQL and NewSQL information stores to give a point of view on the field, offering bearing to pros and administrators to pick fitting most far off point procedures, and seeing pesters and openings in the field. An appraisal among the most noticeable techniques was made on various estimations, including tending to limits information models, security and scaling properties. Conditions and use cases in which NoSQL and NewSQL databases have been utilized were bankrupt down and the reasonableness of two or three responses for various plans of jobs was judged. The talk of the conditions, also as the nearby examination of information stores, will help experts in picking the best conglomerating choices for their needs. In like manner, our work has confirmed difficulties in the area, including anomaly, pathetic relationship, passing on superior to anything normal blend, kept documentation, deficient examination, sporadic pubescence of plans, benchmarking criteria, and nonattendance of help and non-closeness of a systematized deals language.

At long last, as the whimsical idea and hugeness of information is tirelessly making, it is head that the structure with which information is dealt with in like way advances. The Apache Flink is figured out how to resuscitate the way by which information is overseen. Flink expands the MapReduce point of view and is appeared around a cyclic dataflow viewpoint which gives a dull gifted runtime. In like manner, this runtime is crucial to both gathering and gushing information. Flink is along these lines perpetually adaptable on the other hand with Hadoop MapReduce. Plan degrees of movement in Flink - a working memory the experts, a pipelined dataflow, an inline program streamlining administrator, an iterateable runtime - improve execution of information regulating and diminishing the conventional laziness. These recognitions show to make Flank an agent in inescapable predetermination of information arranging.

There is sure adaptability issue of existing sub-tree Anonymization over cloud so proposed Descend Traversal Prioritization (DTP), Ascend Traversal Abstraction (ATA) and crossbreed approach that joins Descend Traversal Prioritization (DTP) and Ascend Traversal Abstraction (ATA) together. DTP gives favored productivity over Top - Down Specialization to the degree execution time .It spares less execution effort for little k-nonappearance of definition respect and at any rate it requires high execution hypothesis for goliath k-absence of clearness plainly ATA improves than Bottom - Up Generalization where it requires less execution experience for tremendous k-riddle and high execution time for little k - namelessness. The cream approach combines both DTP and ATA have been satisfied in an especially versatile way by frameworks for a procedure of intentionally managed Map Reduce occupations. Exploratory outcomes have exhibited that the mutt approach basically revives the flexibility and ampleness of sub-tree data Anonymization complexity to existing systems.

5.2 FUTURE WORK

This domain examines a piece of the conceivable future headings in the field of circled preparing. While it is past the area of innovative personality to would like to anticipate the future heading which is a field of study will look for after, it was conceivable to perceive two or three models recorded as a printed copy, which may propose and manage the course of future research. The future research toward thusly may include:

- In setting of Aneka, there is a probability to finish client depicted programming model that may intertwine GPU empowered programming. Conventional compartments can be worked for empowering cross breed mists to help increment associations in spite of for other cloud vendors. Cloud masters can in like way be executed to keep up coordination between information servers.

- Better security highlights for the cloud clients that may join present day highlights like biometric, complex encryption methods, face based insistence structures can be made to give better underwriting and endorsement of clients
- In-database frameworks including NewSQL highlights can be passed on to give better information get to associations to the cloud clients.
- Further studies utilizing more noteworthy cloud based structures or business legitimate examinations and a logically wide locale and spread of cloud associations can be performed with better cloud middleware usage.

REFERENCES

1. Inmon W. H., *Building the Data Warehouse*, 3rd edition, John Wiley & Sons, 2002.
2. Wei Fan and Albert Bifet. "Mining Big Data: Current Status, and Forecast to the Future", *SIGKDD Explorations*. 14(2).
3. Sachchidanand Singh and Nirmala 2013 International Conferenceon ComputingTechnology (ICCICT). *IEEE*,2011.
4. Singh. Big dataAnalytics", Communication,Information& Stephen Kaisler, Frank Armour, J. Alberto Espinosa, William Money. "Big Data: Issues and Challenges Moving Forward", 46th Hawaii International Conference on (pp. 995-1004).*IEEE*, 2013.
5. Sadhana and Savitha Shetty, "Analysis of Diabetic Data Set Using Hive and R", *International Journal of Emerging Technology and Advanced Engineering*,4(7), 2014.
6. Vikram Phaneendra,S.& E.Madhusudhan Reddy, "Big Data- solutions for RDBMS problems-A survey". In*12th IEEE/IFIP Network Operations & Management Symposium*. 2013.
7. Kiran kumara Reddi & Dnvsl Indira "Different Technique to Transfer Big Data :survey" *IEEE Transactions*. 52(8):2013.
8. Albert Bifet, "Mining Big Data In Real Time" *Informatica* 37.2013.
9. Mrigank Mridul, Akashdeep Khajuria, Snehasish Dutta and Kumar N " Analysis of Bigdata using Apache Hadoop and Map Reduce" https:/ /www.ijarcsse.com/docs/papers/Volume_4/5_May2014/V4I5-0391.pdf
10. Sagiroglu, S. Sinanc,D."Big Data: A Review".*Collaboration Technologies and Systems* (CTS), International Conference on, 42(47):20-24.2013.
11. Garlasu, D.; Sandulescu, V.; Halcu, I. ; Neculoiu, G. A Big Data implementation based on Grid Computing", *Grid Computing*.2013.

12. Wullianallur Raghupathi, Viju Raghupathi. Big data analytics in healthcare: promise and potential. *Health Information Science and Systems*, 2(3): 2-10. 2014.

13. Sahoo. PK, Suvendu Kumar Mohapatra And Shih-Lin Wu, Analyzing Healthcare Big Data With Prediction for Future Health Condition. *IEEE Access*. Vol. 4, 9786-9799; 2016.

14. Islam, S. M. R D. Kwak, M. H. Kabir, M. Hossain, and K.-S. Kwak, The Internet of Things for health care: A comprehensive survey," *IEEE Access*, vol. 3,678-708, 2015

15. Lin, K, F. Xia, W. Wang, D. Tian, and J. Song, "System design for big data application in emotion-aware healthcare", *IEEE Access*, vol. 4, pp. 6901-6909,2016.

16. Tawalbeh L. A, R. Mehmood, E. Benkhlifa, and H. Song, "Mobile Cloud computing model and big data analysis for healthcare applications", *IEEE Access*, vol. 4, pp. 6171-6180, 2016.

17. Dehury C. K and P. K. Sahoo, "Design and implementation of a novel service management framework for iot devices in Cloud", *J. Syst. Softw.*,vol. 119, pp. 149-161, Sep. 2016

18. Yu, Zhiwen; Luo, Peinan; You, Jane; Wong, Hau-San; Leung, Hareton; Wu, Si;Zhang, Jun; Han, Guoqiang., "Incremental semi-supervised clustering ensemble for high dimensional data clustering", *IEEE Trans. Knowl. Data Eng.*, vol. 28, no. 3, pp. 701-714, Mar. 2016.

19. Mukaka. M, "A guide to appropriate use of correlation coefficient in medical research," *Malawi Med. J.*, vol. 24, no. 3, pp. 69-71, 2012.

20. Rallapalli S, R. R. Gondkar, and U. P. K. Ketavarapu, "Impact of processing and analyzing healthcare big data on Cloud computing environment by implementing hadoop cluster," *Procedia Comput. Sci.*, vol. 85, pp. 16-22, May 2016.

21. Huang T, L. Lan, X. Fang, P. An, J. Min, and F. Wang, "Promises and challenges of big data computing in health sciences '', *Big Data Res.*, vol. 2, no. 1, pp. 2-11, 2015.

22. Dean J and S. Ghemawat, "MapReduce: Simplified data processing on large clusters," *Commun. ACM*, vol. 51, no. 1, pp. 107-113, Jan. 2008.

23. Lee M and X. Han, "Complex window query support for monitoring streaming data in wireless body area networks", *IEEE Trans. Consum. Electron.*, vol. 57, no. 4, pp. 1710-1718, Nov. 2011.

24. Ashwin Belle, Raghuram Thiagarajan, S. M. Reza Soroushmehr Fatemeh Navidi, Daniel A. Beard, and Kayvan Najarian, Big Data Analytics in Healthcare *BioMed Research International* Volume 2015, Article ID 370194.

25. McAfee A. E. Brynjolfsson, T. H. Davenport, D. J. Patil, and D. Barton, "Big data: the management revolution," *Harvard Business Review*, vol. 90, no.10, pp. 60–68, 2012.

26. Elshazly H , A. T. Azar, A. El-korany, and A. E. Hassanien, "Hybrid system for lymphatic diseases diagnosis," in *Proceedings of the International Conference onAdvances in Computing,Communications and Informatics (ICACCI '13)*, pp. 343–347, *IEEE*, Mysore, India, August 2013.

27. Dougherty G, *Digital Image Processing forMedical Applications*, Cambridge University Press, 2009.

28. Ritter F, T. Boskamp, A. Homeyer et al."Medical image analysis," *IEEE Pulse*, vol. 2, no. 6, pp. 60–70, 2011.

29. Sobhy D, Y. El-Sonbaty, and M. Abou Elnasr, "MedCloud: healthcare Cloud computing system," in *Proceedings of theInternational Conference for*161–166, *IEEE*, London, UK, December 2012.

30. Wang F, V. Ercegovac, T. Syeda-Mahmood et al."Largescale multimodal mining for healthcare with MapReduce," in BioMed. ResearchInternational *Proceedings of the 1st ACM International Health Informatics Symposium*, pp.479–483,ACM,November 2010.

31. Markonis D, R. Schaer, I. Eggel, H.Muller, andA.Depeursinge, "Using MapReduce for large-scale medical image analysis," in *Proceedings of the 2nd IEEE International Conference on Healthcare Informatics, Imaging and Systems Biology (HISB '12)*, p. 1, IEEE, San Diego, Calif, USA, September 2012.

32. Shackelford K, "System& method for delineation and quantification of fluid accumulation in efast trauma ultrasound images", *US Patent Application,* 14/167,448, 2014.

33. Ohno-Machado L, V. Bafna, A. A. Boxwala et al."iDASH: integrating data for analysis, anonymization, and sharing," *Journal of the AmericanMedicalInformatics Association*, vol. 19,no. 2, pp. 196–201, 2012.

34. Yang C.T, L.-T. Chen, W.-L.Chou, and K.-C. Wang, "Implementation of a medical image file accessing system on Cloud computing," in

Proceedings of the 13th IEEEInternationalConference on Computational Science and Engineering (CSE' 10), pp. 321–326, December 2010.

35. Teng C.-C, J. Mitchell, C. Walker et al."A medical image archive solution in the Cloud," in *Proceedings of the IEEE International Conference on Software Engineering and Service Sciences (ICSESS '10)*, pp. 431–434, *IEEE*, July 2010.

36. Davey J. W, P. A. Hohenlohe, P. D. Etter, J. Q. Boone, J. M. Catchen, and M. L.Blaxter, "Genome-wide genetic marker discovery and genotyping using next-generation sequencing," *Nature Reviews Genetics*, vol. 12, no. 7, pp. 499– 510,2011.

37. Treangen T.J and S. L. Salzberg, "Repetitive DNA and next generation sequencing: computational challenges and solutions," *Nature Reviews Genetics*, vol. 13, no. 1, pp. 36–46, 2012.

38. Koboldt D.C, K.M. Steinberg, D. E. Larson, R. K.Wilson, and E.R. Mardis, "The next-generation sequencing revolution and its impact on genomics," *Cell*, vol. 155, no. 1, pp. 27–38, 2013.

39. Lander E.S, L.M. Linton, B. Birren et al."Initial sequencing and analysis of the human genome," *Nature*, vol. 409, no. 6822, pp. 860–921, 2001.

40. Drmanac R,A. B. Sparks, M. J. Callow et al."Human genome sequencing using unchained base reads on self-assembling DNA nanoarrays," *Science*, vol. 327, no. 5961, pp. 78–81, 2010.

41. Chen R, G.I.Mias, J. Li-Pook-Than et al."Personal omics profiling reveals dynamic molecular and medical phenotypes," *Cell*, vol. 148, no. 6, pp. 1293– 1307, 2012.

42. Dhavapriya, M. and Yasodha, "Big Data Analytics: Challenges and Solutions Using Hadoop, Map Reduce and Big Table", *International Journal of Computer Science Trends and Technology (IJCST)*, 4(1):5-14.2016.

43. Kenn Slagter, Ching-Hsien Hsu "An improved partitioning mechanism for optimizing massive data analysis using MapReduce " Published online: 2013 © Springer Science+Business Media New York.

44. Kyong-Ha Lee Hyunsik Choi "Parallel Data Processing with MapReduce: ASurvey" *SIGMOD Record*, 4(4). 2011.

45. Chen He Ying Lu David Swanson "Matchmaking: A New MapReduce Scheduling" in *10th IEEE International Conference on Computer and Information Technology (CIT'10)*, 2736–2743.2010.

46. Madhavi Vaidya, "Parallel Processing of cluster by Map Reduce", *International Journalof Distributed and Parallel Systems (IJDPS)*.3(1), 2012.

47. Acharjya D.P. and Kauser Ahmed PA. Survey on Big Data Analytics: Challenges, Open Research Issues and Tools, *(IJACSA) International Journal of Advanced Computer Science and Applications*, 7(2), 2016.

48. Mukherjee, A.; Datta, J.; Jorapur, R.; Singhvi, R.; Haloi, S.; Akram, W., "Shared disk big data analytics with Apache Hadoop". 2012.

49. Fayyad, U. M.; Piatetsky-Shapiro, G.; Smyth, P.; and Uthurusamy, R. Advances in Knowledge Discovery and Data Mining. Menlo Park, Calif.: AAAI Press. 1996.

50. Nandakumar, A. N. Nandita Yambem, A Survey on Data Mining Algorithms on Apache Hadoop Platform, *Certified Journal*, 4(1), 2014.

51. Aditya B. Patel, Manashvi , Birla, Ushma Nair. Addressing big data problem using Hadoop and Map Reduce.

52. Harshawardhan S. Bhosale , Devendra P. Gadekar,"A Review Paper on Big Data and Hadoop", *International Journal of Scientific and Research Publications*, Volume 4, Issue 10, October 2014 1 ISSN 2250-3153.

53. Huang Lu, Chen Hai-Shan, Hu Ting-Ting, "Research on Hadoop Cloud Computing Model and its Applications Networking and Distributed Computing" (ICNDC), *Third International Conference*, 2012,

54. Anjan K Koundinya, Srinath N.K,K.A.K. Sharma, Kiran Kumar, Madhu M N,And Kiran U Shanbag,¯Map Reduce Design And Implementation Of APriori Algorithm For Handling Oluminous Data*Advanced Computing: An International Journal (Acij)*, 3(6), 2012.

55. Peter Augustine D., Leveraging Big Data Analytics and Hadoop in Developing India's Healthcare Services, *International Journal of Computer*

56. Ekanayake et al., Twister: a runtime for iterative MapReduce, HPDC ' 10Proceedings of the 19th ACM International Symposium on High Performance Distributed Computing Pages 810-818, 2010.

57. Matei Zaharia, Mosharaf Chowdhury, Michael J. Franklin, Scott Shenker, Ion Stoica. Spark: Cluster Computing with Working Sets.HotCloud 2010. June 2010.

58. Matei Zaharia, Mosharaf Chowdhury, Tathagata Das, Ankur Dave, Justin Ma, Murphy McCauley, Michael J. Franklin, Scott Shenker, Ion Stoica. ResilientDistributed Datasets: A Fault-Tolerant Abstraction for In-Memory Cluster Computing. NSDI 2012. April 2012.

59. Casey Stella, 2014, Spark for Data Science: A Case Study, Basu, Real-Time Healthcare Analytics onApacheHadoopusing

60. Spark MLib, Apache Spark performance,https://spark.apache.org/mllib/.

61. Yan Hu, Fangjie Lu, Israr Khan, Guohua Bai, A Cloud Computing Solution for Sharing Healthcare Information, *The 7th International Conference for Internet Technology and Secured Transactions (ICITST), IEEE,* 2012, London.

62. Nikhita Reddy, G. and G.J.Ugander Reddy, Study of Cloud Computing in, HealthCare Industry.https://arxiv.org › cs 2014.

63. Yan Hu and Guohua Bai, A systematic literature review of Cloud computing in e-health, *Health Informatics, An International Journal (HIIJ),* 3(4):11-20, 2014.

64. Sanjay P. Ahuja1, Sindhu Mani1 & Jesus Zambrano1, A Survey of the State of Cloud Computing in Healthcare, Network and Communication Technologies. *Canadian Centre of Science and Education.* 1 (2): 12-19, 2012.

65. Atiya Parveen, Sobia Habib, Waseem Ahmad, The Cloud changing the Indian healthcare system, *International Journal of Computer Science and Mobile Computing, IJCSMC,* 2(5):238 -243, 2013.

66. Kyle D. Lutes, Ibrahim M.Baggili, Diabetic e-Management System (DEMS),*Proceedings of the Third International Conference on Information Technology: New Generations (ITNG'06), IEEE Computer Society,* 2006.

67. George Hsieh, Rong-Jaye Chen, Design for a Secure Interoperable Cloud-Based Personal Health Record Service,*4th International Conference on Cloud Computing Technology and Science, IEEE,* 472-479,2012.

68. Carlos Oberdan Rolim, Fernando Luiz Koch, Carlos Becker Westphall, Jorge Werner, Armando Fracalossi, Giovanni Schmitt Salvador, A Cloud

Computing Solution for Patient's Data Collection in Health Care Institutions, *Second International Conference on eHealth, Telemedicine, and Social Medicine, IEEE*, 95-99, 2010.

69. Abdullah Al-Malaise Al-Ghamdi, Majda A.Wazzan, Fatimah M. Mujallid, Najwa K. Bakhsh, An Expert System of Determining Diabetes Treatment Based on Cloud Computing Platforms, Abdulla Al-Malaise Al-Ghamdi et al,*/(IJCSIT) International Journal of Computer Science and Information Technologies*, 2(5):1982-1987, 2011.

70. Roma Chauhan, AmitKumar, Cloud Computing for Improved Healthcare:Techniques, Potential and Challenges, *4th IEEE International Conference on E-Health and Bioengineering, Romania*, 21-23, 2013.

71. VisheshVed, VivekTyagi, Ankur Agarwal, A. S. Pandya,Personal Health Record System and Integration Techniques with Various ElectronicMedical RecordSystem, *IEEE 13th International Symposium on High-Assurance Systems Engineering*, 2011.

72. VassilikiKoufi, Flora Malamateniou and George Vassilacopoulos, Ubiquitous Access to Cloud Emergency Medical Services.*IEEE*, 978-1, 2010.

73. Shaftab Ahmedm,M Yasin Akhtar Raja,Role of Social Networking in Patient Monitoring and e-Healthcare, *IEEE*, 978, 2013.

74. Niketan Pansare, Vinayak Borkar, Chris Jermaine, Tyson Condie *"Online Aggregation for Large MapReduce Jobs"* Seattle, VLDB Endowment, ACM. 2011.

75. Sreekanth Rallapalli and Augustin Minalkar Improving Health care-Big Data analytics for Electronic health records on Cloud.*Journal of Advances in Information Technology*,7(1), 2016.

76. Rajesh Jangade and Ritu Chauhan, Big data with integrated Cloud computing for healthcare analytics computing for Sustainable Global Development (INDIA.Com), 2016.

77. Kavitha and S.Kannudurai, "Health Care Analytics With Hadoop Big Data Processing", *International Journal of Advanced Research in Biology Engineering Science and Technology (IJARBEST)* Vol. 2, Special Issue 15, March 2016.

78. Taylor R. A Pare JR, Venkatesh AK, Mowafi H and Melnick., "Prediction of in-hospital mortality in emergency department patients

with sepsis: A local big data driven, machine learning approach," *Acad. Emerg. Med.*, vol. 3, no. 23, pp.269_278, Mar. 2016.

79. Weng C.H, T. C.-K.Huang, and R.-P. Han, "Disease prediction with different types of neural network classifiers," *Telematics Inform.*, vol. 33,no. 2, pp. 277_292, 2016.

80. Li H, X. Li, M. Ramanathan, and A. Zhang, "Prediction and informative risk factor selection of bone diseases", *IEEE/ACM Trans. Comput.Biol.Bioinf.*, vol.12, no. 1, pp. 79-91, Jan./Feb. 2015.

81. Henriques J, Carvalho P, Paredes S, Rocha T, Habetha J, Antunes M, Morais J.Prediction of heart failure decomposition events by trend analysis of tele-monitoring data. IEEE J Biomed Health Inform. 2015 Sep;19(5):1757–1769

82. Gope.P and T. Hwang, "BSN-Care: A secure IoT-based modern healthcare system using body sensor network," *IEEE Sensors J.*, vol. 16, no. 5, pp. 1368- 1376, Mar. 2016.

83. Singh. J, C. Liddy, W. Hogg, and M. Taljaard, "Intracluster correlation coefficients for sample size calculations related to cardiovascular disease prevention and management in primary care practices," *BMC Res. Notes*, vol. 8, no. 1, pp. 1-10, 2015.

84. Prajesh P Anchalia, Anjan K Koundinya, Shrinath N K. "MapReduce Design of K-means Clustering Algorithm", *IEEE*, 2013.

85. Lijun Mei, W.K. Chan, T.H. Tse (2008), -A Tale of Clouds: Paradigm Comparisons and Some Thoughts on Research Issues , *Asia-Pacific Services Computing Conference - IEEE*, pp 464-469.

86. Surbhi Sangwan, Yudhvir Singh (2017), -Services and Security Aspects in Cloud Computing , *International Journal of Computer Science and Information Technology Research Excellence*, Volume 7, Issue 1, Pp 6-9.

87. Sean Carlin, Kevin Curran (2012), -Cloud Computing Technologies , *International Journal of Cloud Computing and Services Science*, Volume1, Issue 2, pp. 59-65.

88. C.Weinhardt, A. Anandasivam, B. Blau, N. Borissov, T. Meinl, W. Michalk, J. Stober (2009), -Cloud Computing – A Classification, Business Models and Research Directions , *Business and Information System Engineering-Springer*, Volume 1, Issue 5, pp 391-199.

89. Michael Hogan, Fang Liu, Annie Sokol, Jin Tong (2013) -NIST Cloud Computing Standards Roadmap , *NIST Special publication*, USA, pp 1-76.

90. Ang Li, Xiaowei Yang, Srikanth Comparing Public Cloud Providers , *measurement*, pp 1-14.

91. Kandula, Ming Zhang (2010), ¯CloudCmp: *10th ACM SIGCOMM conference on Internet*

92. Salman A. Baset (2012), -Cloud SLAs: Present and Future , *ACM SIGOPS Operating Systems Review*, Volume 46, Issue 2, pp 57-66.

93. Kartalopoulos, S.V. (2008), -Differentiating Data Security and Network Security , *IEEE International Conference on Communications*, Beijing, China, pp 1469-1473.

94. Kevin Hamlen, Murat Kantarcioglu, Latifur Khan, Bhavani Thuraisingham (2010), Security Issue for Cloud Computing , *technical report published in "UTDCS-02-10"*.

95. Dowd, P.W., McHenry, J.T. (1998), -Network security: it's time to take it seriously *Computer-IEEE*, Volume 31, Issue 9, pp 24-28.

96. Arshad Hashmi and Omar M. Barukab (2016), -A Survey on Security Patterns and Issues in Cloud Computing Environment , *International Journal of Technical Research and Applications*, Volume 4, Issue 6, pp 59-67.

97. Z. Mahmood (2011), -Data location and security issues in cloud computing *International Conference on Emerging Intelligent Data and Web Technologies Tirana, Albania – IEEE*, pp 49-54.

98. S. Subashini, V. Kavitha (2011), -A survey on security issues in service delivery models of cloud computing , Journal of Network and Computer Applications – IEEE, Volume 34, pp 1–11.

99. L Wei, Haojin Zhu, Zhenfu Cao, Xiaolei Dong, Weiwei Jia, Yunlu Chen,Athanasios V. Vasilakos (2013), -Security and privacy for storage and computation in cloud computing, *Journal of Information Science - Elsevier*, Volume 258, pp 371–386.

100. Hanqian Wu, Yi Ding, Chuck Winer, Li Yao (2010), -Network Security for Virtual Machine in Cloud Computing , *International Conference on Computer Sciences and Convergence Information Technology (ICCIT) – IEEE*, Seoul, South Korea.

101. Zhifeng Xiao and Yang Xiao (2013), -Security and Privacy in Cloud Computing *IEEE Communications Surveys & Tutorials*, Volume 15, Issue 2.

102. G. Ateniese, R. Burns, R. Curtmola, J. Herring, L. Kissner, Z. Peterson, and D. Song (2007), -Provable data possession at Untrusted Stores , *ACM conference on Computer and Communications Security*, Alexandria, Virginia, USA, pp 598-609..

103. Juels and B. S. Kaliski (2007), -PORs: Proofs of retrievability for large files, *ACM conference on Computer and communications security*, Alexandria, Virginia, USA, pp 584-597.

104. G. Ateniese, R. D. Pietro, L. V. Mancini, and G. Tsudik (2008), -Scalable and efficient provable data possession , *international conference on Security and privacy in communication networks* Article 9, Istanbul, Turkey.

105. Erway, A., C. Papamanthou, and R. Tamassia (2009), -Dynamic provable data possession , *ACM conference on Computer and Communications Security*, Chicago, Illinois, USA, pp 213-222.

106. K.D. Bowers, A. Juels, and A. Oprea (2009), -HAIL: A high-availability and integrity layer for cloud storage, *ACM conference on Computer and communications security*, Chicago, Illinois, USA, pp 187-198.

107. S. Gritzalisa, D. Spinellisc, P. Georgiadisd (1998), -Security protocols over open networks and distributed systems: formal methods for their analysis, design, and verification, *Journal of Computer Communications – Elsevier*, Volume 22, Issue 8, pp 697-709.

108. Mazhar Ali ,Samee U. Khan, Athanasios V. Vasilakos (2015) -Security in cloud computing: Opportunities and challenges , *Information Sciences – Elsevier*, Volume 305, pp 357-383.

109. Schiffman, J., Yuqiong Sun, Vijayakumar, H., Jaeger, T. (2013), -Cloud Verifier: Verifiable Auditing Service for IaaS Clouds , *IEEE ninth World Congress on Services*, Santa Clara, CA, USA, pp 239-246.

110. Pitropakis, N., Darra, E., Vrakas, N., Lambrinoudakis, C. (2013), -It's All in the Cloud: Reviewing Cloud Security , *International Conference on Autonomic and Trusted Computing (UIC/ATC)*, Italy, pp 355-362.

111. Alabool, H.M., Mahmood, A.K. (2014), -Common Trust Criteria For IaaS cloud evaluation and selection , *International Conference on Computer and Information Sciences*, Kuala Lumpur Malaysia, pp 1-6.

112. Hazarika P., Baliga V., Tolety S. (2014), -The mobile-cloud computing (MCC) roadblocks , *International Conference on Wireless and Optical Communications Networks-IEEE*, Bangalore, India, pp 1-5.

113. Madhusudan KL, Dr. Paramashiviah P, Dr. Narahari NS (2013), -Data security issues in Cloud Contact Center as a service – A Review , *International Journal of Innovative Research in Science, Engineering and Technology*, Vol. 2, Issue 3, pp 825-835.

114. Selvakumar, C., Rathanam, G.J., Sumalatha, M.R. (2013), -PDDS - Improving cloud data storage security using data partitioning technique , *IEEE 3rd International Advance Computing Conference*, Ghaziabad, India, pp 7-11.

115. Deyan chen, HongZhao (2012), -Data Security and Privacy Protection Issues in Cloud Computing , *IEEE International Conference on Computer Science and Electronics Engineering*, Hangzhou, China, pp 647-651.

116. Yongzhi Wang, Jinpeng Wei, Srivatsa, M., YucongDuan, Wencai Du (2013), -IntegrityMR: Integrity assurance framework for big data analytics and management applications , *International Conference on Big Data*, Silicon Valley, CA, USA, pp 33-40.

117. Gibson, J., Rondeau, R., Eveleigh, D., Qing Tan (2012), -Benefits and challenges of three cloud computing service models , *International Conference on Computational Aspects of Social Networks*, Sao Carlos, Brazil, pp 198-205.

118. Dimitrios Zissis, Dimitrios Lekkas (2010), -Addressing cloud computing security issues , *Future Generation Computer Systems - Elsevier*, Volume 28, Issue 3, pp 583-592.

119. Gowrigolla, B., Sivaji, S., Masillamani, M.R. (2010), -Design and auditing of Cloud computing security , *5th International Conference on Information and Automation for Sustainability (ICIAFs)*, Colombo, Sri Lanka, pp 292-297.

120. Wentao Liu (2012), -Research on Cloud Computing Security Problem and Strategy *2nd International Conference on Consumer Electronics, Communications and Networks (CECNet)-IEEE*, Yichang, China.

121. Kumbhare, A., Simmhan, Y., Prasanna, V. (2012), -Cryptonite: A Secure and Performant Data Repository on Public Clouds , *IEEE 5th International Conference on Cloud Computing (CLOUD)*, Honolulu, HI, USA, pp 510-517.

122. Hassan, S., Abbas Kamboh, A., Azam, F. (2014), -Analysis of Cloud Computing Performance, Scalability, Availability and Security , *International Conference on Information Science and Applications (ICISA)-IEEE*, Seoul, South Korea, pp 1-5.

123. Sabetzadeh F., Tsui E., Lee W.B. (2014), -Enhancing knowledge quality via a semantic-oriented framework for a social knowledge cloud , *5th IEEE International Conference on Software Engineering and Service Science (ICSESS)*, Beijing, China, pp 153-156.

124. Fitzek, F.H.P., Toth, T., Szabados, A., Pedersen, M.V., Lucani, D.E., Sipos, M., Charaf, H., Medard, M. (2014), -Implementation and performance evaluation of distributed cloud storage solutions using random linear network coding , *IEEE International Conference on Communications Workshops (ICC)*, Sydney, NSW, Australia, pp 249-254.

125. Abbdal, S.H., Hai Jin, Deqing Zou, Yassin, A.A.(2014), -Secure and Efficient Data Integrity Based on Iris Features in Cloud Computing , *7th International Conference on Security Technology (SecTech)-IEEE*, Haikou, China, pp 3-6.

126. Philip Derbeko, Shlomi Dolev, Ehud Gudes, Shantanu Sharma, -Security and privacy aspects in MapReduce on Clouds: A survey , *Computer Science Review-Elsevier*, Volume 20, May 2016.

127. Koushik Annapureddy (2010), -Security Challenges in Hybrid Cloud Infrastructures . *Seminar on Network Security*, Aalto University,.

128. Francis, R.R. (2012), -Reliability of cloud computing in Quantum Chemistry calculations , *International Conference on Cloud Computing Technologies, Applications and Management (ICCCTAM)*, Dubai, United Arab Emirates, pp 119-120.

129. Reddy, Y.B. (2014), -Cloud-Based Cyber Physical Systems: Design Challenges and Security Needs , *10th International Conference on Mobile Ad-hoc and Sensor Networks (MSN)*, Maui, HI, USA, pp 315-322.

130. G. Zacharia, A. Moukas and P. Maes. (2000), -Collaborative Reputation Mechanisms for Electronic Marketplaces , *Decision Support Systems - Elsevier*, Volume 29, Issue 4, pp 7-29.

131. Nix, R., Kantarcioglu, M., Shetty, S. (2013), -Toward a Real-Time Cloud Auditing Paradigm , *IEEE Ninth World Congress on Services (SERVICES)*, Santa Clara, CA, USA, pp 255-259.

132. Changji Wang, Xuan Liu, Wentao Li (2012), -Implementing a Personal Health Record Cloud Platform Using Ciphertext-Policy Attribute-Based Encryption , *4th International Conference on Intelligent Networking and Collaborative Systems (INCoS)*, Bucharest, Romania, pp 8-14.

133. Paudel, S., Tauber, M., Brandic, I. (2013), -Security Standards Taxonomy for Cloud Applications in Critical Infrastructure IT , *8th International Conference for Internet Technology and Secured Transactions (ICITST)-IEEE*, London, UK, pp 645-646.

134. Pecchia, A., Cotroneo, D., Ganesan, R., Sarkar, S. (2014), -Filtering Security Alerts for the Analysis of a Production SaaS Cloud , *7th International Conference on Utility and Cloud Computing - IEEE*, London, UK, pp 233-241.

135. Abolfazli, S., Sanaei, Z., Ahmed, E., Gani, A., Buyya, R. (2014), -Cloud-Based Augmentation for Mobile Devices: Motivation, Taxonomies, and Open Challenges, *IEEE Communications Surveys & Tutorials*, Volume: 16, Issue: 1, pp 337-368.